Grade 5

Carson-Dellosa Publishing LLC
Greensboro, North Carolina

Credits
Content Editor: Bitsy Griffin
Copy Editor: Elise Craver

Visit *carsondellosa.com* for correlations to Common Core, state, national, and Canadian provincial standards.

Carson-Dellosa Publishing LLC
PO Box 35665
Greensboro, NC 27425 USA
carsondellosa.com

ISBN 978-1-4838-4164-9
02-224191151

Table of Contents

Math 4 Today: Daily Skill Practice is a comprehensive yet quick and easy-to-use supplement to any classroom math curriculum. This series will strengthen students' math skills as they review numbers, operations, algebraic thinking, measurement, data, and geometry.

This book covers 40 weeks of daily practice. Essential math skills are reviewed each day during a four-day period with an assessment of the skills practiced on the fifth day. Each week includes a math fluency practice section, intended to be a quick one-minute activity that encourages fluency in math facts. For more detailed fluency tips, see pages 5 and 6. The week concludes with a math journal prompt.

Various skills and concepts are reinforced throughout the book through activities that align to the state standards. To view these standards, see the Standards Alignment Chart on page 7.

Indicates the daily fluency skill

Indicates the weekly practice page

Indicates the weekly assessment

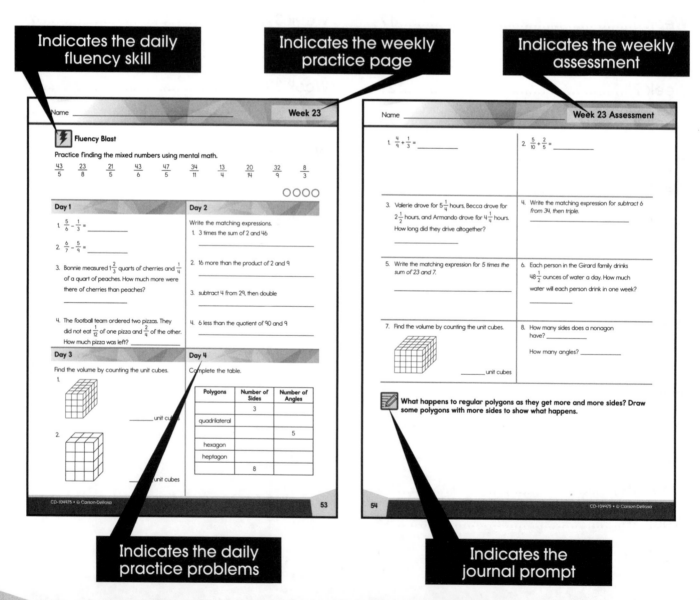

Indicates the daily practice problems

Indicates the journal prompt

Developing Fluency

One of the primary goals of every teacher is to help students learn basic math facts accurately, recall them fluently, and retain that fluency over time. Fluency is the stage of learning where the learner acquires the information at an automatic level. A student must have this fluency of math facts in order to perform multi-digit algorithms and problem solve efficiently.

Math strategies should be introduced and reinforced daily to develop number sense. Opportunity is lost to develop number sense when math facts are taught only through rote memorization. The key to using strategies for basic facts is to have students discover the patterns in addition and multiplication and name them. For example, in addition, students may recognize doubles facts. In multiplication, students may see that 1 times any number equals the same number.

The ability to effortlessly recall math facts lessens students' anxiety and increases their confidence when engaging in more challenging math tasks.

Math Fluency Activities

Use these fun and easy games to engage students in practicing math facts.

- **Dice Roll**—Roll two dice. Use the numbers to practice adding, subtracting, multiplying, dividing, and creating fractions.
- **Flash Card Swat**—Using flash cards, students flip over two cards at a time. Students should use a flyswatter to swat a card they think they know the answer to and say the answer.
- **Race the Room**—Tape a long piece of bulletin board paper to a wall. Have teams of students stand on the opposite side of the room. Say math facts and have students race to the paper and write the answers.
- **War**—Using a deck of cards, students flip over two cards and add (or multiply). Whoever says the correct sum (or product) first keeps the cards.

Using the Fluency Blast

The fluency blast section is designed for students to use mental math on a daily basis. It is not intended that students write the answers each day. Students should practice the fluency blast facts for the week every day (excluding assessment day). Have students color a bubble for each day of practice. Begin the activity by setting a timer for one minute (or 30 seconds). To ensure students are practicing the math facts accurately, post an answer key on the first day.

Tracking Fluency

Have students use the reproducible on page 6 to track their progress. First, students should set a time for when they would like to meet their fluency goals. Then, they should fill in the blank spaces with the math facts they would like to practice. Finally, have students color a section as they master each goal. This page can be used monthly, quarterly, or throughout the entire school year.

Name _____

Fact Fluency Blastoff!

My goal is to know all of my _____facts

by _____.

I know
all of my
_____
facts!

Fact

Fact

Fact

Fact

Fact

Fact

Fact

Fact

Fact

Fact

Fact

Standards Alignment Chart

State Standards*		Weeks
Operations and Algebraic Thinking		
Write and interpret numerical expressions.	5.OA.1, 5.OA.2	1, 4, 5, 8, 9, 12, 13, 16, 17, 20, 21, 24, 25, 28, 29, 32, 33, 36, 37, 40
Analyze patterns and relationships.	5.OA.3	2, 4, 6, 8, 10, 12, 14, 16, 18, 20, 22, 24, 26, 28, 30, 32, 34, 36, 38, 40
Number and Operations in Base Ten		
Understand the place value system.	5.NBT.1–5.NBT.4	1, 5, 9, 13, 17, 21, 25, 29, 33, 37
Perform operations with multi-digit whole numbers and with decimals to hundredths.	5.NBT.5–5.NBT.7	2, 6, 10, 14, 18, 22, 26, 30, 34, 38
Number and Operations—Fractions		
Use equivalent fractions as a strategy to add and subtract fractions.	5.NF.1, 5.NF.2	3, 7, 11, 15, 19, 23, 27, 31, 35, 39
Apply and extend previous understandings of multiplication and division to multiply and divide fractions.	5.NF.3–5.NF.7	4, 8, 12, 16, 20, 24, 28, 32, 36, 40
Measurement and Data		
Convert like measurement units within a given measurement system.	5.MD.1	1, 5, 9, 13, 17, 21, 25, 29, 33, 37
Represent and interpret data.	5.MD.2	2, 6, 10, 14, 18, 22, 26, 30, 34, 38
Geometric measurement: understand concepts of volume and relate volume to multiplication and division.	5.MD.3–5.MD.5	3, 4, 7, 8, 11, 12, 15, 16, 19, 20, 23, 24, 27, 28, 31, 32, 35, 36, 39, 40
Geometry		
Graph points on the coordinate plane to solve real-world and mathematical problems.	5.G.1, 5.G.2	1, 2, 4–6, 8–10, 12–14, 16–18, 20–22, 24–26, 28–30, 32–34, 36–38, 40
Classify two-dimensional figures into categories based on their properties.	5.G.3, 5.G.4	3, 7, 11, 15, 19, 23, 27, 31, 35, 39

The research is clear that family involvement is strongly linked to student success. Support for student learning at home improves student achievement in school. Educators should not underestimate the significance of this connection.

The fluency activities in this book create an opportunity to create or improve this school-to-home link. Students are encouraged to practice their math fluency facts at home with their families each week. Parents and guardians can use the reproducible tracking sheet (below) to record how their students performed in their fluency practice during the week. Students should be encouraged to return their tracking sheets to the teacher at the end of the week.

In order to make the school-to-home program work for students and their families, it may be helpful to reach out to them with an introductory letter. Explain the program and its intent and ask them to partner with you in their children's educational process. Describe the role you expect them to play. Encourage them to offer suggestions or feedback along the way.

Name _____ Week of _____

Fact Fluency: Practice Makes Perfect!

Day	Fact(s) I practiced	How I practiced	How I feel about these facts
M		☐ flash cards ☐ worksheet ☐ game ☐ other _____	☺ ☐ ☹
T		☐ flash cards ☐ worksheet ☐ game ☐ other _____	☺ ☐ ☹
W		☐ flash cards ☐ worksheet ☐ game ☐ other _____	☺ ☐ ☹
Th		☐ flash cards ☐ worksheet ☐ game ☐ other _____	☺ ☐ ☹

CD-104975 • © Carson-Dellosa

Fluency Blast

Practice using mental math.

2 × 4	25 ÷ 5	6 × 6	16 ÷ 4	9 × 3	10 ÷ 2
9 × 8	90 ÷ 9	2 × 5	8 × 6	6 ÷ 3	2 × 2

○○○○

Day 1

1. Write **four hundredths** in standard form.

   _____

2. $20 \times 10^3 =$ _____

3. Compare the numbers using <, >, or =.

   0.007 ◯ 0.07

4. Round 5.67 to the nearest tenth. _____

5. What is the value of the **4** in 745? _____

Day 2

1. $(7 + 8) + (56 \div 7) =$ _____

2. $(21 \div 7) \times 4 =$ _____

3. The area of a rectangular roof on a birdhouse is 56 square inches. If the length of the roof is 8 inches, how wide is the roof in inches?

   _____

Day 3

1. 6 g = _____ mg

2. 2 m = _____ cm

3. 500 mL = _____ L

4. Cody's bedroom has a perimeter of 46 feet. If the length of the bedroom is 11 feet, what is the width of the bedroom in yards?

   _____

Day 4

Graph and label each ordered pair.

1. A (3, 4)
2. B (1, 8)
3. C (5, 1)

Identify the following points found on the graph.

4. D (_____, _____)
5. E (_____, _____)

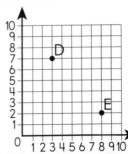

Name _____

1. 5 g = _____ mg

2. $(8 + 1) \times 5 =$ _____

3. Compare the numbers using <, >, or =.

    22.59 $\bigcirc$ 2.259

4. $6 + (6 - 2) \times 6 =$ _____

5. Round **264.1** to the nearest ten.

    _____

6. Fernando collected 245 cans for the school can drive. He gave 35 cans to each of his two sisters to take to their classes. How many cans did he have left to take to his class?

    _____

7. The perimeter of the roof is 216 inches. The length of the roof is 63 inches. How many inches wide is the roof?

    _____

8. Graph each pair of coordinates.
    (4, 4) (1, 2) (5, 2) (7, 5)

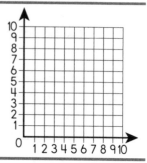

 How does the use of parentheses, brackets, and braces help you solve math problems?

CD-104975 • © Carson-Dellosa

Fluency Blast

Practice using mental math.

6 × 7	81 ÷ 9	8 × 2	12 ÷ 6	4 × 7	9 × 3
28 ÷ 2	27 ÷ 3	3 × 4	14 ÷ 7	7 × 9	5 × 3

○○○○

Day 1

1. 70,000 ÷ 7,000 = _____

2. 762 ÷ 6 = _____

3. $\begin{array}{r} 54.45 \\ + 19.26 \\ \hline \end{array}$

4. Iman spent $7.25 for spaghetti and meatballs, $1.42 for a bottle of water, and $4.75 for dessert. How much did Iman spend for her entire dinner? _____

5. Julio bought a shirt for $58.98. The sales tax was $3.54. How much did Julio spend on his shirt? _____

Day 2

Paige spends 15 minutes cleaning her fish tank every 5 days.

1. Complete the table.

Days	Minutes Cleaning
5	15
10	
15	
20	
25	

2. On what day had Paige spent an hour cleaning the fish tank? _____

Day 3

1. Put the following fractions in order from least to greatest: $\frac{1}{3}, \frac{1}{4}, \frac{1}{3}, \frac{1}{2}, \frac{1}{3}, \frac{1}{4}, \frac{1}{2}, \frac{1}{8}, \frac{1}{8}, \frac{1}{4}, \frac{1}{3}, \frac{1}{2}$.

_____

2. Create a line plot using the fractions in problem 1.

⟵—————————————⟶

3. Which fraction occurs the most? _____

4. Which fraction occurs the least? _____

Day 4

1. Graph the data from the table on day 2.

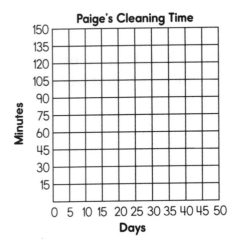

2. On what day do you predict that Paige will have spent 2 hours cleaning the fish tank? _____

1. $11 \times 8 =$ _____

    $40 \div 8 =$ _____

2. $2.30
    + $1.43

3. Marisa bought shoes for $48.34. The sales tax was $3.38. How much did Marisa spend on her shoes? _____

4. $5.54 + $0.48 = _____

5. How many tenths are in the number **54.724**?
    _____

6. Create a line plot using the fractions.

    $\frac{1}{8}, \frac{1}{2}, \frac{1}{4},$

    $\frac{1}{3}, \frac{1}{3}, \frac{1}{3},$

    $\frac{1}{4}, \frac{1}{2}$

7. While swimming, Kenan took 2 breaths on lap 2, 3 breaths on lap 4, and 4 breaths on lap 6. Use this information to complete the chart.

Laps	Breaths
2	2
4	
6	
8	
10	

8. Graph the data from problem 7 on the coordinate plane.

    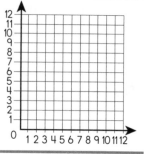

 Why is it helpful to put data on a line plot? What kinds of questions can you answer when numbers are in order?

Fluency Blast

Practice using mental math.

8 × 4	35 ÷ 7	4 × 5	6 × 2	3 × 6	36 ÷ 6
9 × 7	16 ÷ 2	2 × 3	25 × 5	72 ÷ 9	7 × 6

○○○○

Day 1

1. Tony bakes a casserole for $25\frac{5}{12}$ minutes. He decides it needs to bake longer. He bakes it for another $2\frac{3}{6}$ minutes. How long does the casserole bake altogether? _____

2. $\frac{2}{4} + \frac{3}{8} =$ _____

3. $\frac{3}{6} + \frac{1}{3} =$ _____

4. $\frac{7}{12} - \frac{2}{4} =$ _____

5. If $\frac{3}{10} = \frac{30}{100}$, then $\frac{4}{10} = \frac{}{100}$.

Day 2

1. Shane has $60.00 in his wallet. He buys a basketball for $12.89 and a sled for $39.99. How much money does he have left? _____

2. $7 \times 4 + 8 - 2 =$ _____

3. Write a matching expression for *double 7, multiply 3 and 1, then subtract the second number from the first number.*

_____

Day 3

1. 500 cm = _____ mm

2. 2,500 g = _____ kg

3. 48 m = _____ mm

4. Maggie and Stan collected 8 kilograms of canned goods. How many grams did they collect? _____

Day 4

1. Color the quadrilaterals.

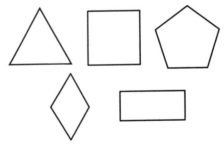

2. Use the figure to describe the attributes of a rectangle.

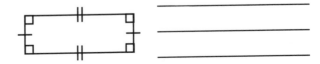

_____

_____

_____

1. $\frac{5}{12} + \frac{1}{4} =$ _____

2. $\frac{3}{8} + \frac{1}{2} =$ _____

3. Uma is making a stir-fry. She measures $\frac{5}{8}$ cup of chicken and then adds $\frac{1}{4}$ cup more. How much chicken does Uma use altogether?

_____

4. If $\frac{4}{10} + \frac{5}{100} = \frac{45}{100}$, then $\frac{7}{10} + \frac{7}{100} = \frac{}{100}$.

5. Round **2.377** to the nearest hundredth.

_____

6. Compare the numbers using <, >, or =.

1.975 $\bigcirc$ 1.97

7. 12 c. = _____ pt.

8. Use the figure to describe the attributes of a parallelogram.

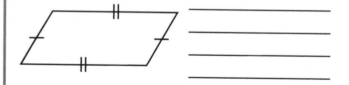

_____
_____
_____
_____

 Explain the difference between regular and irregular polygons.

Fluency Blast

Practice using mental math.

2 × 9	72 ÷ 9	5 × 4	8 ÷ 2	9 × 6	6 × 4
3 × 9	56 ÷ 8	7 × 5	10 × 9	56 ÷ 7	4 × 4

○○○○

Day 1

1. $\frac{3}{8} + \frac{1}{4} =$ _____

2. $\frac{4}{5} - \frac{1}{4} =$ _____

3. $\frac{4}{9} - \frac{1}{3} =$ _____

4. 81.38
   + 2.77
   _____

5. 31.10
   − 3.05
   _____

Day 2

1. Javier is going to mow the common area. It is 14 yards by 7 yards. What is the area that Javier will mow? _____

2. Kit collects $1.24 every day. How much money does she have after 10 days? _____

3. Write a matching expression for *multiply 9 and 5 and then subtract 15.*

   _____

Day 3

Use the line plot to answer the questions.

Lengths of Sticks in Inches

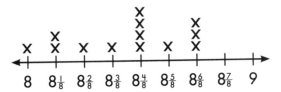

1. How many sticks were part of the data set?
   _____

2. How many sticks are shorter than 8.75 inches?
   _____

3. A craft project calls for sticks that are 8.25 inches to 8.75 inches long. How many sticks can be used for the project? _____

Day 4

1. Name three kinds of parallelograms to complete the hierarchy.

   quadrilateral
   ↓
   parallelogram
   ↓

   _____

   _____

   _____

1. 54.45
   + 19.26

2. Draw a model to show how to add $\frac{1}{6}$ and $\frac{1}{3}$.

3. 32.84
   − 21.25

4. Brady makes 2 goody bags for a party. If each goody bag weighs $\frac{7}{8}$ ounces, how many ounces do the goody bags weigh in all?

   _____

5. Catherine has to carry 9 grocery bags into the house. Each grocery bag weighs 16 pounds. How many pounds does Catherine carry in all?

   _____

6. Add the data to the line plot.

   $8\frac{1}{8}$, $8\frac{1}{8}$, 8,

   9, $8\frac{5}{8}$, $8\frac{3}{8}$,

   $8\frac{5}{8}$, $8\frac{1}{4}$

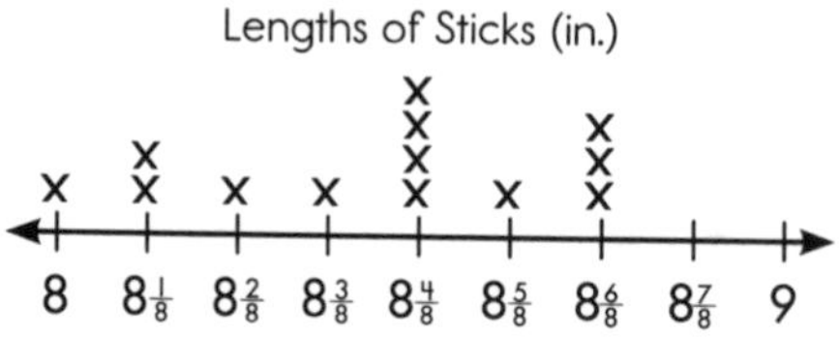

   Lengths of Sticks (in.)

   ```
                        x
                        x        x
        x      x        x        x
   x    x  x   x    x   x    x   x
   <--+--+--+--+--+--+--+--+--+-->
      8  8⅛ 8⅖ 8⅜ 8⅘ 8⅝ 8⅚ 8⅞ 9
   ```

7. Using the information in problem 6, how many sticks are 8.25 inches to 8.75 inches long?

   _____

8. What are the three main types of triangles?

   _____

   _____

   _____

Can you subtract 18.64 from 30? Why or why not?

Name _____

  Fluency Blast

Practice using mental math.

4 × 5	36 ÷ 6	7 × 3	64 ÷ 8	8 × 5	56 ÷ 8
3 × 5	49 ÷ 7	6 × 10	63 ÷ 7	2 × 7	54 ÷ 9

○○○○

Day 1

1. Round **3.047** to the nearest hundredth.
   _____

2. Write **thirty-six thousandths** in standard form.
   _____

3. What is the value of **2** in 2,553? _____

4. Compare the numbers using <, >, or =.

   10.05 ◯ 10.005

5. Write **900,000 + 80,000 + 500 + 7** in standard form.
   _____

Day 2

Write the matching expressions.

1. multiply 4 and 5 and then add 12
   _____

2. double the product of 4 and 7
   _____

3. Denise rented a bike for $12 for a month. She earned $31 a week for delivering newspapers. How much money did Denise have if she delivered newspapers for 3 weeks?
   _____

Day 3

1. 12 qt. = _____ pt.

2. 3 mi. = _____ yd.

3. 3 ft. = _____ in.

4. Jared ran 4.8 kilometers, and Gavin ran 3.7 kilometers. How many meters did they run altogether?
   _____

Day 4

Graph and label each ordered pair.

1. A (2, 9)

2. B (10, 7)

3. C (6, 9)

Identify the following points found on the graph.

4. D (_____, _____)

5. E (_____, _____)

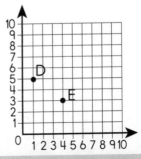

Name _____

1. Compare the numbers using <, >, or =.

    0.99 ◯ 0.09

2. Round **9.921** to the nearest hundredth.

    _____

3. Write **eleven hundredths** in standard form.

    _____

4. Write the matching expression for *the product of 4 and 4 added to double the number 5.*

    _____

5. What is the value of **9** in 215.9? _____

6. Norman used 3 gallons of gas each time he went to the grocery store. He used 2 gallons of gas each time he went to the bank. If he went to the grocery store twice and the bank three times, how many quarts of gas did he use?

    _____

7. 1,200 mm = _____ m

8. Graph each pair of coordinates.
   (4, 1) (2, 9) (6, 7) (8, 10)

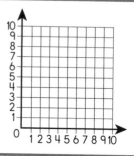

 What is a rule that helps you remember how to round? Does the rule always work? Give examples to show whether it always works.

Fluency Blast

Practice using mental math.

| 7 × 4 | 9 × 2 | 3 × 8 | 6 × 3 | 24 ÷ 3 | 5 × 5 |

| 20 ÷ 4 | 9 × 4 | 14 ÷ 2 | 8 × 7 | 18 ÷ 2 | 12 ÷ 3 |

○○○○

Day 1

1. 264 ÷ 2 = _____

2. 232
    × 4
    _____

3. 13.8
    + 6.9
    _____

4. Kelly buys a book for $9.95. Michael buys a pair of socks for $7.45. How much more money does Kelly spend than Michael?

    _____

Day 2

Complete the table.

1.

Input	−5
61	56
62	
63	
64	
65	

2. What will the number be when the input is 78?

    _____

Day 3

1. Mr. Diaz asked his students what fraction of an hour they spend talking on their cell phones each night. Use the data to create a line plot.

    $\frac{1}{2}, \frac{1}{4}, \frac{1}{2}, \frac{1}{4}, \frac{3}{4}, \frac{1}{4}, \frac{1}{2}, \frac{3}{4}$

    ⟵——————————⟶

2. What is the least amount of time spent on the phone? _____

    The most? _____

3. What is the difference between the two times?

    _____

Day 4

Use the coordinate plane to decide which ordered pair represents the position of each location.

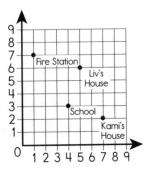

1. Kami's House (_____ , _____)

2. Fire Station (_____ , _____)

3. School (_____ , _____)

4. Liv's House (_____ , _____)

1. Mrs. Patel recorded how many miles each of her students ran during PE class. Use the data to create a line plot.

$$\frac{3}{4}, \frac{1}{4}, \frac{1}{2}, \frac{3}{4}, \frac{1}{2}, \frac{1}{2}, \frac{1}{4}, \frac{3}{4}, \frac{1}{4}, \frac{1}{2}, \frac{1}{4}, \frac{3}{4}$$

2. Scott has $14.35 left in his wallet. He spent $148.43 on tablecloths. He spent $92.05 on napkins. How much money did Scott have in his wallet to start with?

_____

3. How many times greater is the value of the digit 7 in 752.221 than the value of the digit 7 in 904.728?

_____

4. $14 - (0.30 + 0.6) =$ _____

5. Complete the table.

Input	+5
51	
52	
53	
54	
55	

6. $28 \times 12 =$ _____

   $648 \div 8 =$ _____

7. Explain one way that Kami can get to the fire station.

   _____
   _____
   _____
   _____

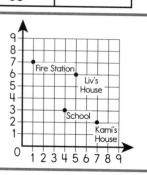

 How does using a coordinate plane help you give directions? Use the coordinate plane to plot your house or school and one place you like to visit. Then, write the directions from your house or school to that place.

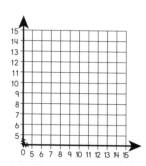

Fluency Blast

Practice using mental math.

3×12	$20 \div 5$	5×6	9×9	$48 \div 8$	2×4
6×6	$24 \div 2$	$15 \div 3$	4×3	$24 \div 4$	8×8

○○○○

Day 1

1. $13\frac{5}{8} + \frac{7}{8} =$ _____

2. $\frac{3}{4} - \frac{5}{10} =$ _____

3. $\frac{8}{12} - \frac{1}{3} =$ _____

4. Sam ate $\frac{1}{4}$ of an apple. Zane ate $\frac{1}{4}$ of the same apple. How much of the apple did Sam and Zane eat altogether? _____

Day 2

1. $(6 \times 2) + 8 =$ _____

2. $3 + (8 \times 2) =$ _____

3. $14 \div 2 + 3 =$ _____

4. $(8 \times 6) - 8 =$ _____

5. $24 \div 4 + 9 =$ _____

Day 3

1. Nikki's square quilt measures 99 inches on each edge. How many yards of trim does she need to buy to go around the perimeter of the quilt?

   _____

2. Parker is 6 feet, 2 inches tall. His brother is 4 feet, 9 inches tall. How many inches taller is Parker than his brother?

   _____

3. 8 oz. = _____ lb.

Day 4

1. What kinds of lines are shown?

   _____

2. Draw a quadrilateral with exactly one right angle.

3. How many of each angle are in this shape?

   acute _____

   obtuse _____

   right _____

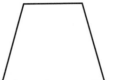

Name _____

1. Luke needs $\frac{1}{2}$ deck of cards for a magic trick. A standard deck of cards has 52 cards in it. If Luke has 22 cards, does he have enough for his trick? Explain. _____
_____

2. $1\frac{3}{4} - \frac{7}{10} =$ _____

3. $8\frac{1}{2} + 7\frac{1}{4} =$ _____

4. $(10 + 10) \div 2 =$ _____

5. $6 \times (3 + 3) =$ _____

6. $10 \times 10 \div 25 =$ _____

7. Kelsey made 8 quarts of soup on Monday, 5 quarts on Tuesday, and 5 quarts on Wednesday. If she serves each guest 1 cup of soup, how many guests can she serve in all?
_____

8. Draw a set of perpendicular lines.

 Sasha drew a shape that had 3 unequal angles. What shape could Sasha have drawn? Draw some examples of shapes that have 3 unequal angles.

Fluency Blast

Practice using mental math.

| 9×9 | $32 \div 8$ | 4×6 | 8×3 | $32 \div 4$ | $70 \div 7$ |

| 7×4 | $21 \div 3$ | 2×6 | $12 \div 2$ | 3×2 | 6×8 |

○○○○

Day 1

1. $4\frac{3}{5} = \frac{}{5}$

2. $\frac{4}{10}$
   $+ \frac{3}{10}$

3. $\frac{1}{2}$
   $+ \frac{1}{5}$

4. Leo and Oliver have to clean their bedrooms. Oliver cleans his room in $\frac{3}{4}$ of an hour. Leo takes twice as long as Oliver. How long did it take Leo to clean his room? _____

Day 2

1. Maddie has 762 feet of ribbon for a project. Isabella has 56 feet, and Jenna has 32 feet. How many yards of ribbon do the three girls have combined? _____

2. Neil drove for 8 hours. Hannah drove for $7\frac{1}{2}$ hours, and Ivan drove for 3 hours. How many minutes did Neil, Hannah, and Ivan spend driving altogether? _____

3. $(2 \times 7) - (2 \times 5) =$ _____

Day 3

1. Complete the table.

m	cm
2	200
5	
8	
11	
14	

2. How many centimeters are in 100 meters? _____

Day 4

Use the coordinate grid to answer the questions.

1. What is the name of the polygon shown?

   _____

2. What are the coordinates of the polygon?

   _____

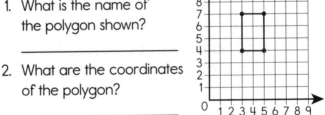

3. Slide the polygon down so that the coordinates of the bottom-left vertex are at (3, 3). What are the polygon's new coordinates?

   _____

1. $3\frac{5}{8} = \frac{}{8}$

2. A hamburger weighs $\frac{1}{3}$ of a pound and an order of french fries weighs $\frac{1}{4}$ of a pound. How much does the entire meal weigh?

   _____

3.
   $$2\frac{1}{2}$$
   $$+\ 3\frac{2}{5}$$
   _____

4.
   $$4\frac{2}{3}$$
   $$-\ 2\frac{1}{6}$$
   _____

5. Ashton changed the oil in his car. It required 6 quarts of oil. If Ashton wants to change the oil in his car every month for a year, how many gallons of oil will he need?

   _____

6. Cindy's swimming pool requires 4 quarts of a bacteria-cleaning agent 5 times a month. How many gallons of this agent will Cindy use during June, July, and August?

   _____

7. 380 mm = _____ m

8. Which coordinate is shared by the triangle and the rectangle?

   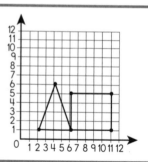

 You have a full container of your favorite drink. Several friends come over. What kind of information do you need to make sure that you give the same amount of drink to each friend?

Fluency Blast

Practice using mental math.

4 × 3	7 × 7	4 ÷ 2	2 × 5	48 ÷ 8	4 × 8
72 ÷ 9	3 × 7	5 × 8	8 ÷ 2	6 × 9	48 ÷ 6

○○○○

Day 1

1. Write **3.6** in word form.

    _____

2. Compare the numbers using <, >, or =.

    62.381 ◯ 62.831

3. What is the value of the **5** in 0.865?

    _____

4. 30×10^4 = _____

5. Round **93.0129** to the nearest thousandth.

    _____

Day 2

1. (2.3 × 5) + 8 = _____

2. $\{[3 \times (4 + 6)] - 8\} + [4 \times (24 - 17)]$ = _____

3. Adam collected 1 seashell a day for 9 days. Braden collected 2 seashells a day for 14 days. How many more seashells did Braden collect than Adam?

    _____

Day 3

1. 48 in. = _____ ft.

2. 6.5 T = _____ lb.

3. 12 ft. = _____ yd.

4. Felicia paints a bookcase. She uses $1\frac{5}{6}$ cups of paint on the outside of the bookcase and $\frac{2}{3}$ cup of paint on the inside. How many pints of paint did Felicia use? _____

Day 4

Graph and label each ordered pair.

1. A (3, 5)
2. B (7, 8)
3. C (1, 3)

Identify the following points found on the graph.

4. D (_____ , _____)
5. E (_____ , _____)

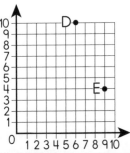

1. Write **1.08** in word form.

   _____

2. Compare the numbers using <, >, or =.

   0.004 ◯ 4.00

3. 20×10^5 = _____

4. $(4 + 6) \div (9 - 4)$ = _____

5. $\{[(9 + 3) \div 2] - 2\} \times [3 \times (14 - 5)]$ = _____

6. Demetri had 5 math problems a day for 25 days. Grey had 7 problems a day for 14 days. How many more math problems did Demetri have than Grey?

   _____

7. 14,000 lb. = _____ T

8. Graph each pair of coordinates.

   (3, 2) (10, 4) (5, 8) (6, 1)

   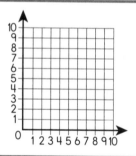

 Why is it important to be able to move between the word, expanded, and standard forms of a number?

⚡ Fluency Blast

Practice using mental math.

5 × 4	21 ÷ 7	9 × 5	5 × 7	7 × 8	81 ÷ 9
8 × 4	66 ÷ 3	4 × 2	12 ÷ 3	28 ÷ 4	3 × 3

○○○○

Day 1

1. 746
   × 5

2. 729 ÷ 9 = _____

3. 12.05
   + 5.06

4. Irene buys a pair of shoes for $51.49 and a board game for $17.65. She pays with four $20 bills. How much change does she get back?

   _____

Day 2

Complete the table.

1.

Input	−3
11	8
12	
13	
14	
15	

2. What will the number be when the input is 20?

   _____

Day 3

1. Jason conducts a survey of his friends to find out what fraction of their money they spend on clothes. Use the data to create a line plot.

   $\frac{1}{8}, \frac{5}{8}, \frac{3}{4}, \frac{7}{8}, \frac{1}{4}, \frac{1}{4}, \frac{1}{8}, \frac{5}{8}, \frac{1}{8}, \frac{3}{4}$

   ⟷

2. How many people spend the smallest fraction of their money on clothes? _____

3. What is the largest fraction of money spent on clothes? _____

Day 4

1. Graph the following coordinates on the coordinate plane. Then, connect the points. What polygon did you make? _____

   (3, 5) (5, 8) (7, 5) (5, 2)

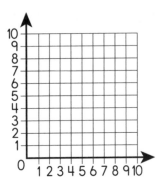

2. Add a point that would make the figure a pentagon. What point did you add? _____

1. This line plot shows the amount of punch in each student's glass. How much punch would be in each glass if the total amount of punch were redistributed equally?

   _____

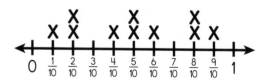

Punch in Glasses (pt.)

---

2. Hestor buys a scooter for $26.99. Zeb buys a basketball for $12.89. How much more money does Hestor spend than Zeb?

   _____

3. Round **46.895** to the nearest tenth.

   _____

---

4. 0.18 × 0.6 = _____

5. Complete the table.

Input	×4
1	4
2	
3	
4	
5	

---

6.   218   46.02
   × 8   + 75.67

7. Graph and connect the points in the order they are listed.

   (2, 6) and (6, 6)

   (2, 1) and (6, 1)

   (4, 6) and (4, 1)

   What letter did you make? _____

   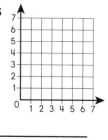

 When you are adding or subtracting decimals, explain why it is important to line up the decimals first.

Fluency Blast

Practice finding equivalent fractions using mental math.

$\frac{1}{2} = \frac{}{4}$ $\frac{3}{8} = \frac{}{16}$ $\frac{2}{3} = \frac{}{12}$ $\frac{3}{4} = \frac{}{8}$ $\frac{3}{5} = \frac{}{20}$

○○○○

Day 1

1. If $\frac{4}{5} = 4 \times \frac{1}{5}$, then $\frac{5}{12} =$ _____ $\times$ ___ .

2. $\frac{8}{10} - \frac{1}{6} =$ _____

3. $9\frac{3}{10} + 7\frac{1}{5} =$ _____

4. Grace and Laura are collecting canned goods. Grace collected $\frac{3}{4}$ of a box of canned goods. Laura collected $\frac{5}{8}$ of a box of canned goods. How much did the girls collect altogether?

   _____

Day 2

1. $(17 - 7) \div 5 =$ _____

2. $10 \div 5 + 3 =$ _____

3. $(15 \div 3) \times 5 =$ _____

4. $(20 \div 5) \times 2 =$ _____

5. $50 \times 2 + 5 =$ _____

Day 3

1. Bill surveyed different teams at school to find out how many of each liked banana muffins. Use the data to create a line plot.

   $\frac{3}{10}, \frac{5}{10}, \frac{4}{10}, \frac{7}{10}, \frac{5}{10}, \frac{4}{10}, \frac{4}{10}, \frac{3}{10}, \frac{8}{10}, \frac{4}{10}, \frac{5}{10}$

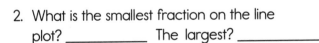

2. What is the smallest fraction on the line plot? _____ The largest? _____

3. What is the difference between the largest and smallest fractions? _____

Day 4

Classify each triangle as **isosceles**, **scalene**, or **equilateral**.

1.   2.

   _____   _____

3.   4.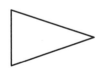

   _____   _____

1. Andre is making several recipes of cakes and cookies for a bake sale. He needs baking soda in the following teaspoon measurements. Place these measurements on the line plot.

   How much total baking soda does Andre need for all of his recipes? _____

   $$\frac{1}{4}, \frac{1}{2}, \frac{1}{4}, \frac{1}{8}, \frac{1}{2}, \frac{3}{4}, \frac{1}{8}, \frac{1}{2}, \frac{3}{4}, \frac{1}{4}$$

   ⟵——————————————⟶

2. Mona swims $\frac{3}{5}$ of a mile farther than Nathan. If Nathan swims $2\frac{4}{10}$ miles, how many miles does Mona swim? _____

3. $15 - (2 + 8) =$ _____

4. $(40 \div 5) - 7 =$ _____

5. $(5 \times 7) - 30 =$ _____

6. $6\frac{3}{4} - 2\frac{3}{12} =$ _____

   $5\frac{1}{2} + 3\frac{1}{3} =$ _____

7. Draw an isosceles triangle. Label the sides and angles to prove it is an isosceles triangle.

Explain the process of adding mixed numbers.

Name _____

 Fluency Blast

Practice using mental math.

3×10^2 $\qquad$ 8×10^3 $\qquad$ 6×10^3 $\qquad$ 4×10^5 $\qquad$ 5×10^3

1×10^4 $\qquad$ 2×10^2 $\qquad$ 7×10^6 $\qquad$ 9×10^7 $\qquad$ 1.2×10^3

○○○○

Day 1

1. $\frac{1}{3} + \frac{2}{5} =$ _____

2. $\frac{4}{5} + \frac{7}{8} =$ _____

3. $\frac{3}{4} + \frac{1}{3} =$ _____

4. $\frac{1}{6} + \frac{2}{5} =$ _____

Day 2

1. Complete the table.

Input	−20
151	131
152	
153	
154	
155	

2. What number will you get when the input is 1,000?

_____

Day 3

1. William buys 9 gallons of ice cream for his party. He has 34 guests coming. If each guest eats $2\frac{1}{2}$ cups of ice cream, how many cups of ice cream will be left?

_____

2. Nora bottles $4\frac{1}{8}$ quarts of barbecue sauce. Later, she bottles another $5\frac{7}{8}$ quarts of barbecue sauce. How many 1-cup servings of barbecue sauce does she have in bottles?

_____

Day 4

1. What is the name of the polygon?

_____

2. What are the coordinates of the polygon?

_____

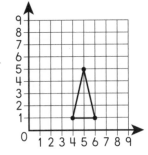

3. Slide the polygon so that the coordinates of the bottom-right vertex are at (9, 4). What are the polygon's new coordinates?

_____

1. $\frac{2}{7} + \frac{3}{14} =$ _____

2. $\frac{2}{3} + \frac{1}{2} =$ _____

3. $\frac{1}{4} + \frac{1}{5} =$ _____

4. $\frac{4}{7} + \frac{1}{3} =$ _____

5. Dawn can paint $\frac{4}{5}$ of a wall in 1 hour. How many walls can she paint in 2 hours?

_____

6. Jeremy eats $\frac{2}{5}$ of a pound of peanuts at a ball game. His friends eat $\frac{7}{8}$ of a pound together at the game. How many pounds of peanuts did they eat in all? _____

7. Wallace delivered 7 containers of orange juice to the Apple Tree Restaurant. Each container had 8 quarts of orange juice. How many gallons of orange juice did Wallace deliver?

_____

8. Plot the following coordinates on the coordinate plane. Then, connect the points. (1, 2) (3, 2) (3, 6) (1, 6)

What polygon did you make?

_____

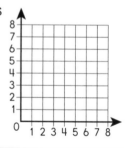

 Think of a time that an improper fraction would be more helpful to you than a mixed number. Explain your reasoning.

Fluency Blast

Practice finding the least common denominator using mental math.

$\frac{3}{4}, \frac{1}{12}$ $\frac{1}{7}, \frac{2}{14}$ $\frac{6}{9}, \frac{1}{3}$ $\frac{6}{7}, \frac{1}{3}$ $\frac{3}{8}, \frac{1}{4}$ $\frac{3}{6}, \frac{11}{18}$ $\frac{4}{5}, \frac{1}{2}$ $\frac{5}{6}, \frac{3}{4}$ $\frac{1}{5}, \frac{4}{15}$ $\frac{2}{3}, \frac{7}{8}$

○○○○

Day 1

1. $400 \div 10^3 =$ _____

2. Round **7.38** to the nearest tenth. _____

3. Write the equivalent decimal.

   $\frac{7}{10} =$ _____

4. How many hundredths are in **45.972**? _____

5. Compare the numbers using <, >, or =.

   6.041 ◯ 6.401

Day 2

Write the matching expressions.

1. double 9 and then add 27 _____

2. add the quotient of 108 and 12 and the quotient of 18 and 2 _____

3. Cara has 252 pieces of candy. She wants to give an equal number of pieces to each student in her class. There are 18 students in her class. How many pieces does each student get?

   _____

Day 3

1. 7 qt. = _____ c.

2. 14,000 lb. = _____ T

3. 8 ft. = _____ in.

4. Gabe's anemometer measures the wind speed at 44.14 kilometers per hour. What is the wind speed in meters per hour?

   _____

Day 4

Graph and label each ordered pair.

1. A (8, 1)

2. B (2, 6)

3. C (10, 3)

Identify the following points found on the graph.

4. D (_____ , _____)

5. E (_____ , _____)

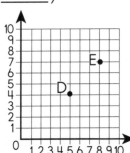

1. $220 \div 10^2 =$ _____

2. Round **5.42** to the nearest tenth. _____

3. Write **4.002** in word form.

   _____

4. Write a matching expression for *the difference of 35 and 7 divided by the difference of 9 and 2.*

   _____

5. Write the equivalent decimal.

   $\dfrac{32}{100} =$ _____

6. Kyle and his father have collected 1,440 coins. They have a coin album that holds 30 coins on each page. If they put the coins in the album, how many pages will they use?

   _____

7. 7 yd. = _____ in.

8. Graph each pair of coordinates.
   (10, 2) (2, 10) (4, 7) (2, 4)

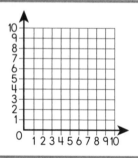

 Explain the pattern involved in moving up in place value from ones to tens to hundreds to thousands. How does that pattern change when you move down each place?

Name _____

 Fluency Blast

Practice reducing fractions to their simplest form using mental math.

$\frac{3}{6}$ $\frac{6}{10}$ $\frac{8}{18}$ $\frac{6}{24}$ $\frac{8}{12}$ $\frac{2}{10}$ $\frac{10}{16}$ $\frac{12}{20}$ $\frac{8}{24}$ $\frac{6}{30}$

○○○○

Day 1

1. 165 ÷ 5 = _____

2. $\begin{array}{r} 16.3 \\ +\ 35.7 \\ \hline \end{array}$

3. 15.02 × 3 = _____

4. Travis ran 5 times as many laps as Reese. If Reese ran 3.7 laps, how many laps did Travis run?

   _____

Day 2

1. Complete the table.

Input	+4
21	25
22	
23	
24	
25	

2. What will the number be when the input is 50?

   _____

Day 3

1. Noah asks his friends what fraction of an hour it takes each of them to get to school. Use the data to create a line plot.

   $\frac{2}{3}, \frac{1}{2}, \frac{1}{2}, \frac{2}{3}, \frac{1}{3}, \frac{1}{2}, \frac{2}{3}, \frac{1}{3}, \frac{2}{3}, \frac{1}{2}, \frac{2}{3}$

2. Which fraction of an hour appears the most?

   _____

3. Which fraction falls in the middle? _____

4. How many of Noah's friends take the shortest amount of time to get to school? _____

Day 4

1. Graph the following coordinates. Then, connect the points. What polygon did you make?
   (3, 1) (5, 8) (9, 8) (7, 1)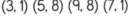

   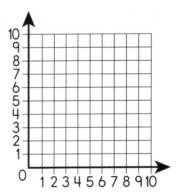

1. Alexis is building a track for her toy train. She needs 3 more feet of track to reach the train station. She has two pieces of track that are $\frac{1}{4}$ foot long, one piece that is $\frac{1}{2}$ foot long, and one piece that is $1\frac{1}{3}$ feet long.

Use the data to create a line plot.

Does Alexis have enough track to reach the station? _____

2. Don finished the race in 5.9 minutes. If Tasha took 4 times as long to finish the race, how many minutes did it take Tasha to finish?

_____

3. How many ounces of macaroni and cheese will each person get if 10 people share 1 pound of the dish?

_____

4. $\{[4 \times (2.1 + 3.9)] - 7\} + [6 \times (6.2 - 4.2)] =$ _____

5. Complete the table.

Input	–4
14	10
15	
16	
17	
18	

6. $\begin{array}{r} 455 \\ \times \ \ 6 \\ \hline \end{array}$ $847 \div 7 =$ _____

7. Graph each pair of coordinates. Then, connect the points. What polygon did you make?
(1, 4) (4, 8) (8, 8) (9, 4)

_____

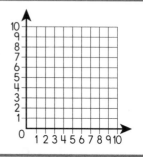

 What steps would you take to shift the polygon in problem 7 to the bottom right of the coordinate plane and keep its shape?

Fluency Blast

Practice finding the least common multiples using mental math.

2, 3	5, 10	3, 4	12, 16	5, 8
18, 24	7, 9	12, 15	8, 10	3, 10

○○○○

Day 1

1. $7\frac{3}{8} - 5\frac{1}{6} =$ _____

2. $12 - (\frac{1}{2} + \frac{2}{3}) =$ _____

3. Jack paints a bookcase. He uses $2\frac{3}{4}$ cups of paint on the outside of the bookcase and $\frac{3}{8}$ cup on the inside of the bookcase. How many cups of paint does Jack use altogether? _____

Day 2

1. $4 \times (4 + 5) =$ _____

2. $(15 \times 2) \div 10 + 8 =$ _____

3. $10 - [(14 \div 2) + 3] =$ _____

4. $(90 \times 1) \div 2 + 7 =$ _____

5. $(45 \div 5) \times 9 - 1 =$ _____

Day 3

1. Holly has 6 gallons of water, and Garrett has 9 quarts. How many pints of water do Holly and Garrett have altogether?

_____

2. Jorge made 12,000 milliliters of orange juice. If he sells 1-liter bottles for $1.09, how much will he earn if he sells all of his juice?

_____

3. Luis measures 3 pieces of string. The first piece is 544 centimeters long, the second piece is 144 centimeters, and the third piece is 113 centimeters. How many meters of string does he have altogether? _____

Day 4

Classify the following triangles based on their angles. Write an **A** on each triangle with only acute angles, an **O** on each triangle with an obtuse angle, and an **R** on each triangle with a right angle.

1. $\frac{1}{3} + \frac{5}{6} =$ _____

2. $\frac{2}{5} - \frac{1}{4} =$ _____

3. Taneshia has eaten $\frac{1}{4}$ of her candy bar. Wayne has eaten $\frac{2}{8}$ of his candy bar. Who has eaten the greater amount? Explain. _____
   _____
   _____

4. $(52 - 16) \div (8 - 4) =$ _____

5. $[4 \times (2 + 2)] + (14 \div 2) =$ _____

6. $[64 - (6 \times 6)] \div (9 - 2) =$ _____

7. Lonnie has 5 feet of string, and Zack has 7 feet of string. How many inches of string do Lonnie and Zack have altogether?
   _____

8. Draw three triangles: one with a right angle, one with an obtuse angle, and one with only acute angles. Label each triangle.

 You need to know if the angles in a building are right angles, but you do not have any measuring devices. How can you determine if the angles are right angles?

Fluency Blast

Practice finding the equivalent fractions using mental math.

$\dfrac{4}{10} = \dfrac{}{20}$　　　　$\dfrac{4}{5} = \dfrac{}{15}$　　　　$\dfrac{1}{7} = \dfrac{}{14}$　　　　$\dfrac{2}{5} = \dfrac{}{25}$　　　　$\dfrac{3}{2} = \dfrac{}{8}$

○○○○

Day 1

1. $\dfrac{1}{3} + \dfrac{5}{6} =$ _____

2. $\dfrac{2}{3} + \dfrac{2}{5} =$ _____

3. $\dfrac{4}{5} - \dfrac{1}{3} =$ _____

4. $\dfrac{3}{4} - \dfrac{5}{8} =$ _____

5. $\dfrac{7}{8} - \dfrac{1}{4} =$ _____

Day 2

1. Ella needs $1\dfrac{1}{2}$ gallons of water to water her plants. Her watering can holds 1 quart. How many times will Ella fill her watering can to water her plants? _____

2. On Saturday, Carlos drives $62\dfrac{1}{4}$ miles each hour. If he travels for 4 hours, how many miles does he travel? _____

Day 3

1. 20 kg = _____ g

2. 5,100 m = _____ km

3. 15 mL = _____ L

4. Richard's favorite hiking trail is 3.5 kilometers long. How many meters long is the trail?

   _____

Day 4

1. Describe the attributes of a trapezoid. _____

   _____

2. Graph each pair of coordinates.
   (2, 4) (4, 4) (3, 8)

   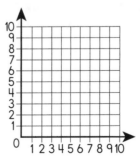

3. Add a point that would make the figure a rhombus. What point did you add? _____

Name _____

1. $\frac{4}{6} \times \frac{1}{3} =$ _____

2. $\frac{1}{4} \times \frac{1}{3} =$ _____

3. Find the area of a rectangle that is 2 feet long and $\frac{4}{5}$ of a foot wide.

   _____

4. $8 \div \frac{1}{3} =$ _____

5. Ms. Jung's art class used $\frac{2}{3}$ of a bottle of blue paint. If they used $\frac{1}{4}$ as much red paint as blue paint, how many bottles of red paint did they use?

   _____

6. Natalie's swimming pool requires 6 quarts of a bacteria-cleaning agent 4 times a month. How many gallons of this agent will Natalie use during July and August?

   _____

7. 4,220 L = _____ kL

8. Graph each pair of coordinates.
   (5, 3) (8, 4) (5, 5)

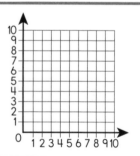

 You have a pack of drawing paper and can give each of your 5 friends 5 pages each. If a sixth friend joins your group, how many pieces of paper will each person get? Show your thinking.

Fluency Blast

Practice using mental math.

10,000 × 24	13 ÷ 1,000	100 × 16	82 ÷ 10	1,000 × 25
16 ÷ 100	82 × 10	25 ÷ 1	100 × 13	24 ÷ 100

○○○○

Day 1

1. Write **seven hundredths** in standard form.
   _____

2. Write **36.14** in expanded form.
   _____

3. Compare the numbers using <, >, or =.

   92.001 ◯ 92.001

4. Round **9.748** to the nearest hundredth.
   _____

5. 70 × 10² = _____

Day 2

Write the matching expressions.

1. four times the difference of ten and eight minus three
   _____

2. 34 minus 5 times the difference of 11 and 16
   _____

3. Maurice ran 15 miles in each of 55 track meets. He ran 10 miles each in another 18 meets. How many miles did Maurice run altogether?
   _____

Day 3

1. 2 mi. = _____ ft.

2. 15 yd. = _____ in.

3. 30,000 lb. = _____ T

4. James used 5 gallons of gas. How many quarts of gas did he use?
   _____

Day 4

Graph and label each ordered pair.

1. A (4, 10)
2. B (9, 1)
3. C (6, 5)

Identify the following points found on the graph.

4. D (_____ , _____)
5. E (_____ , _____)

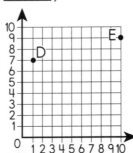

1. Write **108.92** in expanded form.

   _____

2. Compare the numbers using <, >, or =.

   0.08 ◯ 0.80

3. Round **62.686** to the nearest hundredth.

   _____

4. $[2 \times (2 \times 0.75)] \times (4.5 + 1.3) =$ _____

5. Write a matching expression for *the quotient of 16 minus 2 and 7 minus 5.*

   _____

6. Lauren bought a new rack for her CDs and DVDs. The rack has 8 shelves that will hold 16 CDs and 5 shelves that will hold 12 DVDs. How many CDs and DVDs will the rack hold altogether? _____

7. 2 gal. = _____ qt.

8. Graph each pair of coordinates.
   (4, 6), (7, 10), (4, 2), (7, 5)

   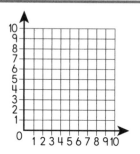

What process do you use when you have to compare two numbers? Show your thinking.

Fluency Blast

Practice reducing each fraction to its lowest terms using mental math.

$\dfrac{21}{24}$ $\dfrac{5}{20}$ $\dfrac{20}{24}$ $\dfrac{3}{36}$ $\dfrac{12}{40}$ $\dfrac{8}{10}$ $\dfrac{15}{18}$ $\dfrac{15}{27}$ $\dfrac{4}{8}$ $\dfrac{8}{20}$

○○○○

Day 1

1. 758
   × 93

2. 2,466 ÷ 3 = _____

3. 3.288
   ×   8

4.   2.89
   + 2.60

5. Gavin's anemometer measures the wind speed at 44.14 kilometers per hour, 4 times faster than the wind speed 5 hours ago. What was the wind speed five hours ago?

   _____

Day 2

1. Complete the table.

Input	+3
35	38
36	
37	
38	
39	

2. What will the number be when the input is 102?
   _____

Day 3

Lengths of Strings (in.)

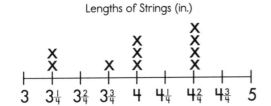

1. How many pieces of string are there?

   _____

2. How many pieces of string are 4 inches or longer? _____

3. What fraction of the string is exactly 3, 4, or 5 inches long? _____

Day 4

List the coordinates for each location.

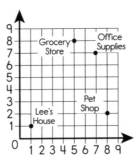

1. Lee's House (_____ , _____)

2. Grocery Store (_____ , _____)

3. Office Supplies (_____ , _____)

4. What is one possible way that Lee can get from his house to the Pet Shop? _____

1. Add the new data to the line plot.

   $3\frac{3}{4}$, 3, $4\frac{3}{4}$, $3\frac{3}{4}$

   Could all of the lengths of string been cut from a 5-foot piece of string? Why or why not? _____

   _____

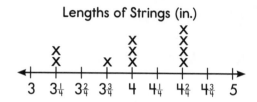

Lengths of Strings (in.)

---

2. Mark ran 2.4 times as many miles as Emory. If Emory ran 2.08 miles, how many miles did Mark run?

   _____

3. $0.20 ÷ 5 =$ _____

---

4. Graph and connect the points in the order they are listed. (2, 5) and (2, 1), (2, 5) and (5, 5), (2, 3) and (3, 3), (2, 1) and (5, 1)

   What letter did you make?

   _____

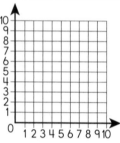

5. Complete the table.

Input	−6
40	34
41	
42	
43	
44	

---

6. $428 × 27 =$ _____

   $34.4 ÷ 4 =$ _____

7. List the coordinates of the Pet Shop.

   (_____, _____)

   What is one possible way that Lee can get from the Grocery Store to Office Supplies? _____

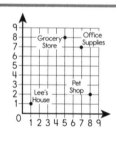

Sketch your first initial on the coordinate plane. What directions would you have to give so that someone else could draw it?

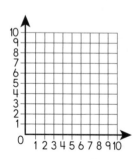

Fluency Blast

Practice finding the least common multiples using mental math.

5, 7	6, 5	8, 7	7, 10	2, 9
6, 10	4, 9	6, 7	3, 10	4, 6

○○○○

Day 1

1. $\frac{1}{3} - \frac{1}{5} =$ _____

2. $\frac{1}{10} + \frac{10}{12} =$ _____

3. $\frac{7}{10} + \frac{1}{5} =$ _____

4. Ben harvested $\frac{7}{10}$ of the potato crop in the morning. After lunch, he harvested $\frac{3}{7}$ of the potato crop. How much more of the crop did Ben harvest in the morning? _____

Day 2

1. $\{(5 \times 5) + [(10 \div 2) + 4]\} - 25 =$ _____

2. $6 + [9 + (9 - 3)] =$ _____

3. $13 + [14 \div (9 - 2)] =$ _____

4. $[36 + (11 - 3)] =$ _____

5. $\{(7 \times 7) + [(9 \div 3) + 6]\} + 12 =$ _____

Day 3

1. 117,000 g = _____ kg

2. 4 qt. = _____ pt.

3. 10 ft. 2 in. = _____ in.

4. Quinton drove 52 minutes on Monday. He drove 25 minutes on Tuesday and 108 minutes on Wednesday. How many hours did Quinton spend driving altogether? _____

Day 4

1. A rectangle has a perimeter of 25 inches. The width is 4.5 inches. What is the length?

_____

2. The bottom edge of an isosceles triangle is 12 centimeters. If the perimeter is 44 centimeters, what is the length of the other sides?

_____

3. The perimeter of a square is 38 inches. What is the length of one side?

_____

Name _____

1. $\frac{5}{12} + \frac{1}{4} =$ _____

2. $\frac{2}{3} - \frac{1}{8} =$ _____

3. Molly's family walked $\frac{5}{6}$ of a hiking trail. John's family walked $\frac{5}{8}$ of another trail that is the same length. Which family walked farther?

   Explain your answer. _____
   _____

4. $(28 \div 4) \times (9 - 1) =$ _____

5. $(10 \times 3) \div (5 - 2) =$ _____

6. $72 \div (4 + 8) =$ _____

7. 5 yd. = _____ ft.

8. A rhombus has a perimeter of 54 centimeters. What is the length of each side? _____

 A rectangle has a perimeter of 60 inches. What are some possible combinations for the lengths and widths of the sides? How do you know?

⚡ Fluency Blast

Practice finding the greatest common factors using mental math.

3, 9	10, 30	15, 25	27, 18	35, 49
54, 90	15, 30	5, 20	49, 70	6, 24

○○○○

Day 1

1. $2 \times \dfrac{1}{2} =$ _____

2. $\dfrac{3}{4} + \dfrac{1}{6} =$ _____

3. $\dfrac{1}{2} \times \dfrac{5}{8} =$ _____

4. Kasey makes fruit juice each morning. She uses $2\dfrac{1}{3}$ pints of strawberries and $1\dfrac{2}{5}$ pints of grapes in her juice. How many more pints of strawberries than grapes does she use?

   _____

Day 2

1. $(41 - 5) \div (7 - 4) =$ _____

2. $(1.8 \times 0.5) \times (3.4 + 2.6) =$ _____

3. $(16 \div 8) + [(15 - 2) \times 9] =$ _____

4. $(42 \div 7) + [(18 - 5) \times 3] =$ _____

5. $(2.0 \times 0.5) \times (1.9 + 3.5) =$ _____

Day 3

1. Dion is shipping two boxes. The first box weighs 4,180 grams, and the second box weighs 820 grams. If the shipping costs $6.43 per kilogram, how much will Dion spend on shipping?

   _____

2. Travon's flight was 180 minutes one way. How many hours did he spend flying round-trip?

   _____

3. 10 pt. = _____ qt.

Day 4

1. Name a quadrilateral that has exactly one set of parallel sides. _____

2. Name a triangle that has exactly two equal sides. _____

3. Name a quadrilateral with two sets of congruent sides that are connected by a vertex.

   _____

1. $\frac{4}{5} \times 7 =$ _____

2. $3 \div \frac{1}{4} =$ _____

3. How much will each person get if 4 people share $\frac{1}{2}$ pound of grapes equally? _____

4. $\frac{1}{12} \times \frac{4}{5} =$ _____

5. At the clothing store, $\frac{1}{8}$ of the clothes are shirts. Of the shirts, $\frac{1}{4}$ are green. What fraction of the clothing in the store are green shirts?

_____

6. Riley rode his bike for 360 minutes. If he traveled 2 miles per hour, how many miles did he travel? _____

7. $[4 + (6 \times 3)] - 12 =$ _____

8. Name a quadrilateral with all four sides equal, opposite sides that are parallel, and opposite angles that are equal.

_____

 Draw a rhombus and a square. Compare and contrast their attributes.

Fluency Blast

Practice finding the equivalent fractions using mental math.

$\frac{1}{4} = \frac{2}{}$ $\frac{2}{3} = \frac{8}{}$ $\frac{1}{2} = \frac{7}{}$ $\frac{3}{8} = \frac{9}{}$ $\frac{7}{8} = \frac{49}{}$

○○○○

Day 1

1. _____ hundreds = 50 tens

2. Write **41.32** in expanded form.

   _____

3. Compare the numbers using <, >, or =.

   101.05 ◯ 101.005

4. Round **22.056** to the nearest whole number.

   _____

5. $3,050 \div 10^2 =$ _____

Day 2

1. $(12 \div 2) + (3 \times 3) =$ _____

2. $(5 \times 3 - 1) \div (7 - 5) =$ _____

3. Write an equation and solve.
   Mr. Dolby will write 115 pages of a travel brochure. The index will take up 3 pages. The rest of the pages will be divided into 8 even sections. How many pages will be in each section? _____

Day 3

Find the volume by counting the unit cubes.

1.

   _____ unit cubes

2.

   _____ unit cubes

Day 4

Graph and label each ordered pair.

1. A (8, 3)
2. B (5, 0)
3. C (7, 2)

Identify the following points found on the graph.

4. D (_____ , _____)
5. E (_____ , _____)

1. Round **22.5240** to the nearest whole number.

    _____

2. Compare the numbers using <, >, or =.

    9.50 ◯ 7.50

3. Write **28.93** in expanded form.

    _____

4. 9 + (8 − 2 × 2) = _____

5. 2 × 2 ÷ 2 × 8 = _____

6. Simone's trip was 500 miles long. She drove the same number of miles each day for 3 days. On the fourth day, she drove 101 miles. How many miles did she drive on each of the first 3 days?

    _____

7. Find the volume by counting the unit cubes.

    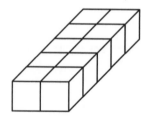

    _____ unit cubes

8. Graph each pair of coordinates.
    (8, 9), (5, 2), (1, 6), (9, 9)

    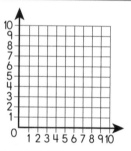

 Make a chart to show what you understand about place value from thousands to thousandths.

Fluency Blast

Practice using mental math.

99 × 10,000   48 ÷ 1,000   54 × 100   65 ÷ 10   91 × 1,000

44 ÷ 100   89 × 10   17 ÷ 1   37 × 1,000   610 ÷ 100

○○○○

Day 1

1. 257
    × 66
    ____

2. 4.545 ÷ 9 = _____

3. Raul mowed three lawns. He deposited $9.50 of his earnings in his savings account. Then, he bought his friend a birthday present for $6.84. When he arrived at the party, he had $4.66 left. How much money did Raul earn mowing lawns? _____

Day 2

1. Complete the table.

Input	+7
50	57
51	
52	
53	
54	

2. What will the number be when the input is 5? _____

Day 3

Find the volume by counting the unit cubes.

1.
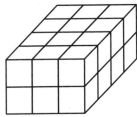

_____ unit cubes

2.
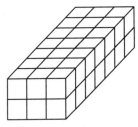

_____ unit cubes

Day 4

Use the coordinate plane to graph the situation. (1 block = 1 grid) Start the trip at Rosa's house at (0, 0). Rosa's mom drives from her house 8 blocks north to the store. Then, they go 4 blocks east for lunch and 6 blocks south for dessert.

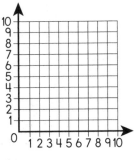

Write the coordinates for each activity.

1. store (_____ , _____)

2. lunch (_____ , _____)

3. dessert (_____ , _____)

4. How many blocks will they have to drive to get back to Rosa's house? _____

1. Use the coordinate plane to graph the situation. (one block = 1 grid) Start the trip at Tiffany's house at (2, 4). On her way to school, Tiffany walked 2 blocks east to her friend's house. Then, they walked together 5 blocks north to buy snacks. Finally, they walked 3 blocks east and 1 block south to get to school.

How far will Tiffany have to walk to get home from school if she makes no stops? _____

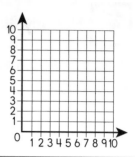

2. A pair of running shoes costs $22.29 for a store to buy from the manufacturer. The store owner wants to make a profit of $18.50. What should be the selling price of the shoes?

_____

3. $0.56 \times 10^5 =$ _____

4. $0.04 \div 0.1 =$ _____

5. Complete the table.

Input	×3
20	60
21	
22	
23	
24	

6. Find the volume by counting the unit cubes.

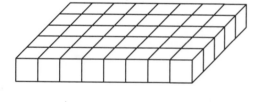

_____ unit cubes

7. $9.89 \times 49 =$ _____

$13.90 + 4.23 =$ _____

 How does finding a pattern for a rule change if you subtract instead of add? Give an example.

Fluency Blast

Practice finding the mixed numbers using mental math.

$\dfrac{43}{5}$ $\dfrac{23}{8}$ $\dfrac{21}{5}$ $\dfrac{43}{6}$ $\dfrac{47}{5}$ $\dfrac{34}{11}$ $\dfrac{13}{4}$ $\dfrac{20}{14}$ $\dfrac{32}{9}$ $\dfrac{8}{3}$

○○○○

Day 1

1. $\dfrac{5}{6} - \dfrac{1}{3} =$ _____

2. $\dfrac{6}{7} - \dfrac{5}{9} =$ _____

3. Bonnie measured $1\dfrac{2}{3}$ quarts of cherries and $\dfrac{1}{4}$ of a quart of peaches. How much more were there of cherries than peaches?

_____

4. The football team ordered two pizzas. They did not eat $\dfrac{1}{12}$ of one pizza and $\dfrac{2}{4}$ of the other. How much pizza was left? _____

Day 2

Write the matching expressions.

1. 3 times the sum of 2 and 46

_____

2. 16 more than the product of 2 and 9

_____

3. subtract 4 from 29, then double

_____

4. 6 less than the quotient of 90 and 9

_____

Day 3

Find the volume by counting the unit cubes.

1.

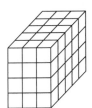

_____ unit cubes

2.

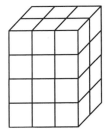

_____ unit cubes

Day 4

Complete the table.

Polygons	Number of Sides	Number of Angles
	3	
quadrilateral		
		5
hexagon		
heptagon		
	8	

Name _____

1. $\frac{4}{9} + \frac{1}{3} =$ _____

2. $\frac{5}{10} + \frac{2}{5} =$ _____

3. Valerie drove for $5\frac{1}{4}$ hours, Becca drove for $2\frac{1}{2}$ hours, and Armando drove for $4\frac{1}{4}$ hours. How long did they drive altogether?

_____

4. Write the matching expression for *subtract 6 from 34, then triple.*

_____

5. Write the matching expression for *5 times the sum of 23 and 7.*

_____

6. Each person in the Girard family drinks $48\frac{1}{2}$ ounces of water a day. How much water will each person drink in one week?

_____

7. Find the volume by counting the unit cubes.

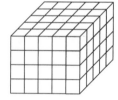

_____ unit cubes

8. How many sides does a nonagon have? _____

How many angles? _____

What happens to regular polygons as they get more and more sides? Draw some polygons with more sides to show what happens.

Name _____

 Fluency Blast

Practice finding the greatest common factors using mental math.

10, 12	9, 21	9, 45	18, 24	12, 30
12, 16	16, 24	30, 25	20, 15	4, 24

○○○○

Day 1

1. $\dfrac{5}{6} \times 4 =$ _____

2. $4 \div \dfrac{1}{10} =$ _____

3. Find the area of a rectangle that is $1\dfrac{3}{10}$ feet wide and 5 feet long. _____

4. Brooke ordered 5 books online. Each book weighed $\dfrac{1}{3}$ of a pound. What was the total weight of Brooke's books? _____

Day 2

1. One-fourth of a bag of popcorn fits in one bowl. How many bowls do you need if you have 6 bags of popcorn?

   _____

2. Delia has eaten $\dfrac{2}{6}$ of her orange. Miguel has eaten $\dfrac{3}{8}$ of his orange. Who has eaten the greater amount? How do you know?

   _____

Day 3

Find the volume of each cube.

1.
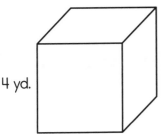
4 yd.

_____

2.
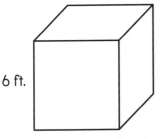
6 ft.

_____

Day 4

1. If a rectangle has a perimeter of 30 feet and a length of 10 feet, what is the width?

2. Graph each pair of coordinates.
   (2, 6) (2, 1) (5, 1)

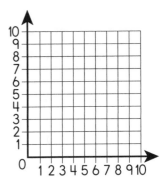

3. Perry's bedroom has a perimeter of 42 feet. If the length of the room is 12 feet, what is the length of the shorter side? _____

1. $\frac{1}{5} \div 5 =$ _____

2. Find the area of a rectangle with a width of $\frac{2}{5}$ of an inch and a length of 5 inches.

   _____

3. How many $\frac{1}{4}$ cup servings are in 4 cups of oatmeal?

   _____

4. $\frac{5}{15} \times \frac{3}{5} =$ _____

5. Maria makes lemonade every morning. She uses $2\frac{1}{4}$ cup of lemon juice and $4\frac{3}{5}$ cups of water. How many cups of water and lemon juice does she use altogether?

   _____

6. Find the volume of the cube.

   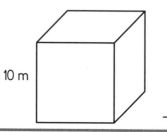

   10 m

   _____

7. Find the volume of the cube.

   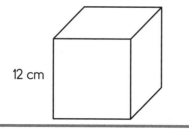

   12 cm

   _____

8. Graph each pair of coordinates.
   (18, 16) (19, 17) (20, 18)

   Based on the pattern, what will the next point on the graph be?

   (_____ , _____)

   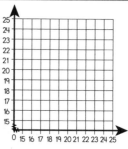

 Look at the pattern found in the points on the graph in problem 8. What is a rule that will help you find other coordinates?

Fluency Blast

Practice finding the missing factors using mental math.

$1 \times$ _____ $= 23$ $4 \times$ _____ $= 44$ $16 \times$ _____ $= 32$ $3 \times$ _____ $= 39$ $9 \times$ _____ $= 45$

$12 \times$ _____ $= 72$ $6 \times$ _____ $= 54$ $2 \times$ _____ $= 142$ $5 \times$ _____ $= 55$ $8 \times$ _____ $= 96$

Day 1

1. $2.5 \times 10^3 =$ _____

2. Write **fifty-seven and one hundred forty-two thousandths** in standard form.

    _____

3. Round **8.876** to the nearest tenth. _____

4. _____ thousands = 90 hundreds

5. Compare the numbers using <, >, or =.

    $214.001 \bigcirc 214.01$

Day 2

1. $\left(\dfrac{1}{3} \times \dfrac{2}{8}\right) + \left(\dfrac{5}{12} - \dfrac{1}{4}\right) =$ _____

2. Write the matching expression for *four times the difference of ten and eight minus three.*

    _____

3. Libby is packaging cookies. She puts 5 cookies each into 400 bags and 8 cookies into 200 bags. She has 3 cookies left over. How many cookies did Libby start with?

    _____

Day 3

Find the volume of each rectangular prism.

1.

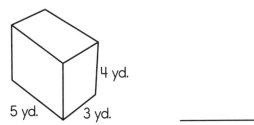

4 yd.

5 yd.   3 yd.   _____

2.

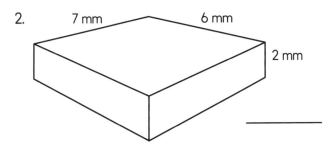

7 mm   6 mm

2 mm

_____

Day 4

Graph and label each ordered pair.

1. A (9, 5)
2. B (0, 8)
3. C (1, 1)

Identify the following points found on the graph.

4. D (_____, _____)
5. E (_____, _____)

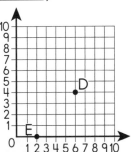

1. Round **6.877** to the nearest tenth.

   _____

2. Write **nine hundred twenty-seven and fifteen hundredths** in standard form.

   _____

3. $1.5 \times 10^2 =$ _____

4. $34 - (6.78 + 2.43) =$ _____

5. Write a matching expression for *add 8 to the sum of 23 and 10.*

   _____

6. Philip is putting doughnuts in boxes. He puts 6 doughnuts each into 350 boxes and 12 doughnuts each into 200 boxes. He has 5 doughnuts left over. How many doughnuts did Philip start with?

   _____

7. Find the volume of the rectangular prism.

   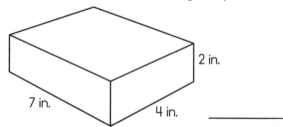

   2 in.

   7 in.

   4 in.   _____

8. Graph each pair of coordinates.
   (10, 6) (1, 10) (5, 3) (7, 7)

   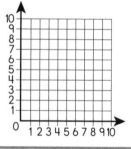

Write a complicated math problem using brackets. Then, write that problem in words. What was easy? What was difficult?

Fluency Blast

Practice finding the equivalent fractions using mental math.

$$\frac{1}{7} = \frac{4}{\underline{}} \qquad \frac{4}{5} = \frac{12}{\underline{}} \qquad \frac{1}{2} = \frac{22}{\underline{}} \qquad \frac{8}{10} = \frac{24}{\underline{}} \qquad \frac{1}{5} = \frac{4}{\underline{}}$$

○○○○

Day 1

1. 67.80 ÷ 10 = _____

2. 410 × 67 = _____

3.　　6.43
　　+ 4.58
　　--------

4. Mason spent $48.74 on new speakers and $25.39 on computer games. After his purchases, he only had $0.58 left. How much money did Mason have before he went shopping?

_____

Day 2

1. Complete the table.

Input	×2
21	42
22	
23	
24	
25	

2. What will the number be when the input is 55? _____

Day 3

Find the volume of each rectangular prism.

1.

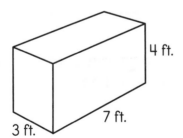

4 ft.

3 ft.　　7 ft.

_____

2.

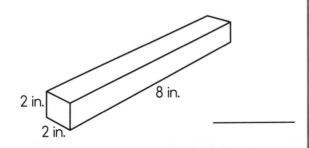

2 in.　　8 in.

2 in.

_____

Day 4

List the coordinates for these locations.

1. Owen's Diner
   (_____ , _____)

2. Park (_____ , _____)

3. Community Pool
   (_____ , _____)

4. Post Office (_____ , _____)

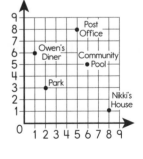

1. 638.07 – 19.34 = _____

2. 426 ÷ 12 = _____

3. Quiana is buying groceries for dinner. Salad costs $4.25, pasta costs $3.15, and bread costs $3.50. How much do Quiana's groceries cost?

_____

4. 1.856 + 2.7 = _____

5. 6.121 × 5 = _____

6. Complete the table.

Input	−3
50	47
52	
54	
56	
58	

7. Find the volume of the rectangular prism.

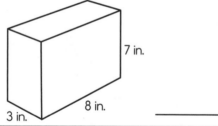

7 in.

8 in.

3 in.

_____

8. What are the coordinates for Nikki's House?

(_____ , _____)

What is one way Nikki could take to get from the pool to the park?

_____

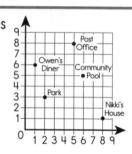

What is another way you can display data from least to greatest other than on a line plot? Compare and contrast your suggestion to a line plot.

Fluency Blast

Practice using mental math.

56×10^4	$87 \div 10^3$	145×10^2	$279 \div 10$	25×10^3
$165 \div 10^2$	807×10	$309 \div 1$	13×10^3	$24 \div 10^2$

○○○○

Day 1

1. $\dfrac{3}{5} + \dfrac{9}{10} =$ _____

2. $\dfrac{2}{3} - \dfrac{1}{6} =$ _____

3. Ann needs $1\dfrac{3}{4}$ yards of fabric to make a dress. She has $4\dfrac{5}{8}$ yards. How many yards of the fabric will be left over? _____

4. Dion and Tory went to buy fruit. Dion bought $\dfrac{3}{4}$ of a pound of grapes. Tory bought $4\dfrac{1}{8}$ pounds of oranges. How many pounds of fruit did they buy in total? _____

Day 2

Write the matching expressions.

1. 8 more than the product of 12 and 4

_____

2. 16 less than the quotient of 200 and 10

_____

3. half the product of 42 and 3

_____

4. 4 times the sum of 53 and 11

_____

Day 3

Use the dimensions to find the volume of each figure.

1. l = 12 centimeters

   w = 4 centimeters

   h = 6 centimeters

   V = _____ cubic centimeters

2. l = 4 meters

   w = 10 meters

   h = 5 meters

   V = _____ cubic meters

Day 4

The sum of the angles in a triangle is 180°. Find the missing angle in each triangle. Then, identify the missing angle as **acute**, **right**, or **obtuse**.

1. 45°, 4°, _____° _____

2. 80°, 60°, _____° _____

3. 55°, 70°, _____° _____

4. 75°, 80°, _____° _____

5. 25°, 65°, _____° _____

1. $\frac{3}{4} + \frac{1}{2} =$ _____

2. $\frac{3}{4} - \frac{1}{12} =$ _____

3. $5 - \frac{3}{5} =$ _____

4. Chang cleans his house in $2\frac{1}{2}$ hours. Jimmy cleans his house in $3\frac{1}{4}$ hours. How much longer does it take Jimmy to clean a house than Chang? _____

5. Write a matching expression for *14 less than the product of 16 and 10.*

    _____

6. Write a matching expression for *the sum of 45 and the product of 3 and 12.*

    _____

7. l = 8 yards

    w = 9 yards

    h = 8 yards

    V = _____ cubic yards

8. Find the missing angle in the triangle.

    85°, 45°, _____°

    Is it right, acute, or obtuse?

    _____

 If the sum of the angles in a triangle is 180°, what do you think the sum of the angles in a quadrilateral will be? Show your thinking.

Fluency Blast

Practice finding the missing factors using mental math.

33 = 11 × _____   42 = 6 × _____   770 = 11 × _____   850 = 85 × _____   175 = 25 × _____

412 = 4 × _____   205 = 5 × _____   1,080 = 20 × _____   300 = 5 × _____   21 = 3 × _____

○○○○

Day 1

1. Shade the area on the grid that shows $\frac{5}{8} \times \frac{2}{4}$.

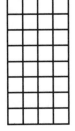

2. $\frac{1}{2} \div 8 =$ _____

3. $\frac{1}{6} \times 5 =$ _____

4. At the grocery store, $\frac{1}{5}$ of the groceries are produce. Of the produce, $\frac{2}{3}$ is vegetables. What fraction of the groceries in the grocery store are vegetables? _____

Day 2

Write the matching expressions.

1. 3 added to 6 times 4 plus 3

_____

2. 16 added to 10 and then divided in half

_____

3. 60 divided by 5 added to 11

_____

4. the difference between the product of 12 and 8 and the sum of 54 and 11

_____

Day 3

Find the volume of each figure.

1.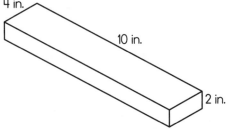

4 in.   10 in.   2 in.

_____

2.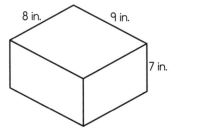

8 in.   9 in.   7 in.

_____

Day 4

Graph each pair of coordinates.

1. (3, 6)

2. (4, 5)

3. (5, 4)

4. (6, 3)

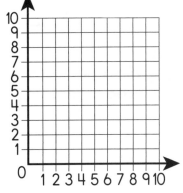

5. What would the next point of the graph be?
(_____ , _____)

1. Shade the area on the grid that shows $\frac{5}{8} \times \frac{2}{4}$.

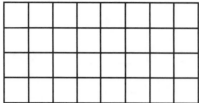

2. $\frac{1}{5} \div 7 =$ _____

3. $\frac{3}{9} \times \frac{3}{7} =$ _____

4. $\frac{1}{8} \div 5 =$ _____

5. Madison puts $3\frac{1}{2}$ quarts of lemonade in a pitcher. She adds another $\frac{1}{2}$ quart. How many pints of lemonade does she have in all?

_____

6. Wendy drove for 540 minutes. If she traveled at 65 miles per hour, how many total miles did she travel?

_____

7. Find the volume of the rectangular prism.

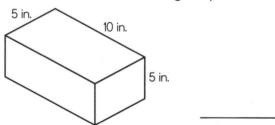

_____

8. Graph each pair of coordinates.

(2, 7) (4, 9) (6, 11)

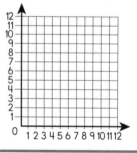

 What happens when you multiply two fractions? Show what happens using an area model.

Fluency Blast

Practice finding the mixed numbers using mental math.

$\frac{16}{10}$ $\frac{12}{8}$ $\frac{9}{6}$ $\frac{21}{8}$ $\frac{17}{6}$ $\frac{20}{18}$ $\frac{22}{17}$ $\frac{20}{3}$ $\frac{13}{8}$ $\frac{14}{4}$

○○○○

Day 1

1. Compare the numbers using <, >, or =.

   0.72 ◯ 0.7

2. Write **54.039** in word form.

   _____

3. 3 hundred = _____ ones

4. $840 \div 10^3 =$ _____

5. Round **4.769** to the nearest hundredth.

   _____

Day 2

1. $(1,392 \div 6) \times (9000 \div 10^3) =$ _____

2. Write a matching expression for *subtract the difference of 20 and 13 from 70.*

   _____

3. Wren is putting bagels into boxes. She puts 8 bagels each into 325 boxes and 12 bagels each into 150 boxes. She has 6 bagels left over. How many bagels did Wren start with?

   _____

Day 3

Find the volume.

1. l = 6.5 cm

   w = 2.5 cm

   h = 4 cm

   V = _____

2. l = 4 km

   w = 5.3 km

   h = 6.5 km

   V = _____

3. 10 pt. = _____ qt.

Day 4

Graph and label each ordered pair.

1. A (7, 2)

2. B (7, 0)

3. C (3, 3)

Identify the following points found on the graph.

4. D (_____ , _____)

5. E (_____ , _____)

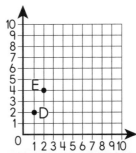

1. 1. $910 \div 10^2 =$ _____

2. Write **187.023** in word form.

   _____

3. Round **27.977** to the nearest hundredth.

   _____

4. $14 - (4 + 3) - 2 =$ _____

5. Write a matching expression for *two-thirds times the sum of two-eights and four-eighths.*

   _____

6. Wyatt is putting basketballs into boxes at a sporting goods store. He puts 12 basketballs each into 118 boxes and 15 basketballs each into 118 boxes. He has 2 basketballs left over. How many basketballs did Wyatt start with?

   _____

7. Virginia needs 48 ounces of charcoal for her grill. How many pounds of charcoal should she buy?

   _____

8. Graph each pair of coordinates.
   (3, 6), (7, 4), (2, 7), (4, 8)

   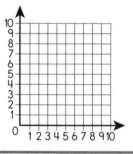

Think about the process of converting between centimeters and meters. What steps do you take? What happens when you convert from millimeters to meters? What changes in your steps?

Fluency Blast

Practice finding the mixed numbers using mental math.

$\frac{8}{5}$ $\frac{15}{4}$ $\frac{7}{3}$ $\frac{5}{2}$ $\frac{10}{3}$ $\frac{6}{5}$ $\frac{15}{7}$ $\frac{20}{9}$ $\frac{3}{2}$ $\frac{17}{4}$

○○○○

Day 1

1. 521.09 – 148.75 = _____

2. 1,160 ÷ 10 = _____

3.   964
   × 83
   _____

4. 131.4 ÷ 3 = _____

Day 2

Tara is making necklaces for her friends. Each necklace takes 25 beads.

1. Complete the table.

Necklaces	Number of Beads
1	25
2	
3	
4	
5	

2. Beads come in packs of 100. How many necklaces can Tara make with one pack?

_____

Day 3

1. Mrs. Becker sells cars. She has some that she needs to ship to another dealership. She is trying to figure out their total weight in tons. Use the data to create a line plot.

$\frac{1}{2}, \frac{1}{8}, \frac{1}{2}, \frac{5}{8}, \frac{1}{4}, \frac{1}{4}, \frac{1}{2}, \frac{3}{4}, \frac{1}{8}, \frac{5}{8}, \frac{1}{4}, \frac{1}{2}$

⟵———————————⟶

2. What is the most common weight? _____

3. What is the lowest weight? _____

4. What is the range of the weights? _____

Day 4

1. Use the table from day 2 to complete the graph.

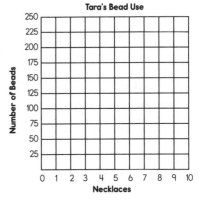

2. What would the next two points on the graph be? (_____ , _____), (_____ , _____)

3. If the beads came in packs of 150, how many necklaces would Tara be able to make with one pack? _____

1. Mrs. Becker has a few more cars than her lot will hold. She wants to move all of the cars that weigh $\frac{5}{8}$ of a ton or more to a warehouse. Use the data to create a line plot.

$\frac{1}{2}, \frac{5}{8}, \frac{1}{2}, \frac{5}{8}, \frac{1}{4}, \frac{3}{4}, \frac{1}{2}, \frac{3}{4}, \frac{1}{8}, \frac{5}{8}, \frac{1}{4}, \frac{1}{2}$

How many cars will she need to move?

_____

⟵——————————————⟶

2. A scale shows the mass of a box of books to be 12.79 kilograms. After removing a book, the mass is 10.98 kilograms. What is the mass of the removed book?

_____

3. 2.110 + 3.55 = _____

4. 0.824 – 0.63 = _____

5. 1,680 ÷ 60 = _____

   187.5 × 5 = _____

6. Ross earns $6 a week for doing chores at home. Complete the table.

Weeks	Amount ($)
1	6
2	
3	
4	
5	

7. Complete the graph with the information from problem 6.

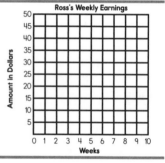

Ross's Weekly Earnings

 Create a survey question such as *How many pages of a book do you read every day?* The answer to your question must be a number. Survey at least 10 people. Display the information on a line plot.

What did you learn? How can you share your information?

Fluency Blast

Practice using mental math.

1.2 × 10   0.28 × 100   5.7 × 1,000   1.04 × 100   0.16 × 100

2.8 × 1,000   2.4 × 10   100 × 1.2   3.05 × 10   3.4 × 1,000

OOOO

Day 1

1. $\frac{1}{3} + \frac{2}{12} =$ _____

2. $4\frac{1}{8} + 5\frac{3}{4} =$ _____

3. $\frac{1}{2}$
    $-\frac{1}{6}$

4. Tia has two packages to mail. Her packages weigh $6\frac{1}{8}$ pounds total. If Tia's first package weighs $4\frac{1}{2}$ pounds, how many pounds does her second package weigh?

    _____

Day 2

Write the matching expressions.

1. 5 times the sum of 3 and itself

    _____

2. 6 increased by 14 divided by 7

    _____

3. 2 times 3 plus 9

    _____

4. 2 less than the product of 5 and 9

    _____

5. 6 less than the sum of 77 and 17, halved

    _____

Day 3

1. Ms. Ferris owns a barn that is 12 yards long, 11 yards wide, and 9 yards high. If Ms. Ferris's barn is rectangular, what is the volume of the barn? _____

2. A toy doll was sent to Lucy in a box that is 8 inches long, 5 inches wide, and 15 inches high. What is the volume of the box?

    _____

3. A swimming pool is 8 meters in length, 6 meters in width, and 3 meters in depth. What is the volume of the swimming pool?

    _____

Day 4

Give two examples of polygons that share the attributes.

1. 4 right angles _____

    _____

2. at least one pair of parallel sides _____

    _____

3. at least one right angle _____

    _____

Name _____

1. $\frac{1}{8} + \frac{3}{16} =$ _____

2. $8\frac{1}{3} + \frac{3}{7} =$ _____

3. $2 - \frac{3}{7} =$ _____

4. Write a matching expression for *10 more than the quotient of 15 and 3.*

   _____

5. Write a matching expression for *2 increased by 6 times 4.*

   _____

6. Write a matching expression for *twice the difference between 8 and 5.*

   _____

7. A moving box is $\frac{1}{2}$ meter long, 1 meter wide, and $\frac{3}{4}$ meter tall. How many cubic meters can the box hold? _____

8. List two polygons that have equal sides.

   _____
   _____

   List two polygons with equal opposite sides.

   _____
   _____

 While sorting shapes in class, Amanda puts a trapezoid in the rectangle pile because it has a right angle. Should the trapezoid be included? Why or why not?

CD-104975 • © Carson-Dellosa

Fluency Blast

Practice using mental math.

0.2	0.08	0.7	0.14	0.06	0.8	0.04	0.2	0.5	0.3
× 4	× 6	× 9	× 2	× 4	× 3	× 5	× 6	× 4	× 5

○○○○

Day 1

1. $\frac{1}{4} \div 3 =$ _____

2. $\frac{4}{6} \times \frac{3}{5} =$ _____

3. Brandy has 8 pounds of candy. She wants to give each of her friends $\frac{1}{3}$ pound. To how many friends can Brandy give candy?

_____

4. Stephan can mow $2\frac{1}{2}$ acres of lawn in 1 day. How many acres of lawn can he mow in $2\frac{1}{3}$ days? _____

Day 2

1. Trolley cars are carrying 1,845 passengers. Each trolley car can hold 40 passengers. How many trolley cars are needed to hold all of the passengers? _____

2. Seth drove 129 minutes on Monday. He drove 98 minutes on Tuesday and 73 minutes on Wednesday. How many hours did Seth spend driving altogether? _____

3. Brianna buys 5 yards of blue fabric. Then, she buys 2 feet of red fabric and 4 feet of green fabric. How many inches of fabric does Brianna buy altogether? _____

Day 3

Find the volume of each figure.

1.

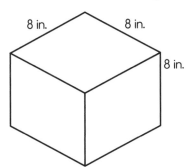

8 in.   8 in.

8 in.

_____

2.

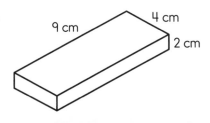

9 cm   4 cm

2 cm

_____

Day 4

Graph the coordinates. Connect them in the order they are listed.

1. (2, 5) and (2, 1)

2. (2, 5) and (4, 3)

3. (4, 3) and (6, 5)

4. (6, 5) and (6, 1)

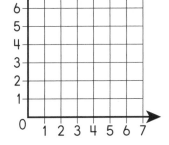

5. What letter did you make? _____

1. $9 \times \dfrac{1}{5} =$ _____

2. $6 \div \dfrac{1}{3} =$ _____

3. $\dfrac{1}{12} \div 4 =$ _____

4. Sally walks $4\dfrac{1}{2}$ miles every day. How many miles does Sally walk in $4\dfrac{1}{2}$ days?

   _____

5. A train is carrying 1,425 passengers. Each of the train cars can hold 30 passengers. How many train cars are needed to hold all of the passengers?

   _____

6. Mr. Hansson cut the grass on the golf course in 1,683 minutes. How many hours did it take him to cut the grass?

   _____

7. Find the volume of the cube.

   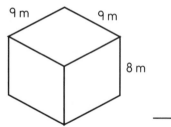

   9 m   9 m   8 m

   _____

8. Graph the coordinate pairs.
   (4, 8) (6, 10) (?, ?) (10, 14)

   Based on the pattern, what is the missing point?
   (_____, _____)

   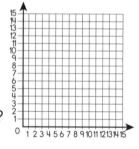

 Explain how to divide a fraction by a whole number. Show your thinking.

Fluency Blast

Practice using mental math.

$9\overline{)2.7}$ $7\overline{)2.1}$ $4\overline{)0.16}$ $8\overline{)5.6}$ $6\overline{)0.30}$ $8\overline{)0.64}$ $9\overline{)0.27}$ $7\overline{)0.28}$ $3\overline{)2.7}$ $9\overline{)5.4}$

○○○○

Day 1

1. Write **45.678** in expanded form.

   _____

2. _____ thousands = 5,000 ones

3. Round **33.01** to the nearest tenth. _____

4. Compare the numbers using <, >, or =.

   0.293 ◯ 0.29

5. $3.5 \times 10^4 =$ _____

Day 2

1. $90 - (3 + 9) \times 7 =$ _____

2. Write a matching expression for *double the product of 6 doubled.*

   _____

3. Sean is packaging tennis balls. He puts 3 tennis balls each into 150 packages and 5 tennis balls each into 75 packages. He has 2 tennis balls left over. How many tennis balls did Sean start with?

   _____

Day 3

Find the volume of each figure.

1.
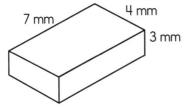
7 mm   4 mm   3 mm

_____

2.
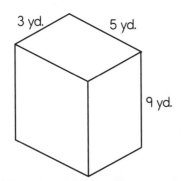
3 yd.   5 yd.   9 yd.

_____

Day 4

Graph and label each ordered pair.

1. A (4, 4)
2. B (5, 2)
3. C (3, 3)

Identify the following points found on the graph.

4. D (_____ , _____)
5. E (_____ , _____)

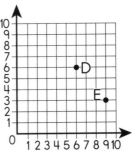

1. $2.7 \times 10^5 =$ _____

2. Round **8.61** to the nearest tenth. _____

3. Write **658.129** in expanded form.

    _____

4. $\left(\frac{2}{3} \times \frac{1}{2}\right) + \left(\frac{2}{3} \div 2\right) =$ _____

5. Write a matching expression for *the sum of the products of 4 and 3 and 1 and 1.*

    _____

6. Clarissa is displaying footballs in a store. She puts 13 footballs each on 8 shelves and 20 footballs each on 5 shelves. She has 11 footballs left over. How many footballs did Clarissa start with?

    _____

7. Find the volume of the rectangular prism.

    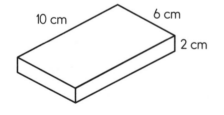

    10 cm   6 cm   2 cm

    _____

8. Graph each pair of coordinates.
    (2, 3), (6, 6), (3, 9), (9, 10)

    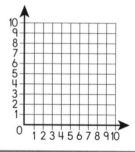

 Create a visual that will help someone else convert between standard measurement units (such as feet to yards).

Fluency Blast

Practice using mental math.

$3\overline{)1.8}$ $2\overline{)0.12}$ $9\overline{)7.2}$ $7\overline{)0.35}$ $4\overline{)0.24}$ $5\overline{)2.5}$ $4\overline{)0.36}$ $9\overline{)6.3}$ $6\overline{)4.8}$ $8\overline{)0.56}$

○○○○

Day 1

1. $2.7 \div 9 =$ _____

2. $\begin{array}{r} 56.14 \\ \times \quad 4 \\ \hline \end{array}$

3. The height of the water in a barrel is 49.27 centimeters. After one month, due to evaporation, the height of water in the barrel is 29.52 centimeters. How much did the water decrease in height during the month?

    _____

Day 2

Dave checks out 4 books from the library every other week. He likes to keep track of how many books he has read.

1. Complete the table.

Weeks	Number of Books
1	4
3	
5	
7	
9	

2. How many books will Dave have read in week 15? _____

Day 3

Elizabeth is making costumes for the school play. She finds scrap ribbon that she might be able to use and enters the lengths on the line plot below.

Ribbon for Costumes (in.)

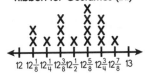

1. How many pieces of ribbon does she have?

    _____

2. Elizabeth needs 12 pieces of ribbon that are at least $12\frac{1}{2}$ inches long each. Does she have enough for the costumes? _____

3. If she needed 13 pieces of ribbon, how long would the shortest piece be? _____

Day 4

1. Graph the information from the table on day 2.

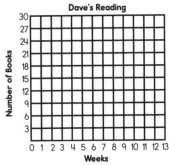

Dave's Reading

Answer the questions based on the pattern you see in the graph.

2. In what week will Dave have read 25 books?

    _____

3. In what week will he have read 40 books?

    _____

1. Elizabeth finds more scrap ribbon that she may be able to use for the costumes. Add the new lengths to the line plot.

   $12\frac{1}{8}, 12\frac{3}{4}, 12\frac{7}{8}, 12\frac{1}{4}, 12\frac{3}{4}, 12\frac{5}{8}$

   How long will the shortest piece be if Elizabeth needs 15 pieces? _____

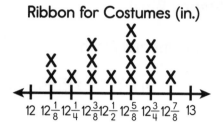

Ribbon for Costumes (in.)

2. The amount of snow Craig measured last November was 21.23 inches. In December, the snowfall was 25.67 inches. How much more snow was there in December than in November? _____

3. $6 \times (4 + 4) \div 2 =$ _____

4. $0.16 \div 2 =$ _____

5. $5.09 - 0.95 =$ _____

   $3.583 + 8.552 =$ _____

6. Yuri spends 20 minutes every other day practicing his guitar. Complete the table to show how long he practices.

Days	Time (min.)
1	20
3	
5	
7	
9	

7. Complete the graph with the information in problem 6.

   How many days does it take for Yuri to have practiced 2 hours?

   _____

   Yuri's Guitar Practice

How would the information in problems 6 and 7 change if Yuri changed his practice time from 20 minutes every other day to 25 minutes? Show your thinking.

Fluency Blast

Practice using mental math.

3.67×10^4 $68 \div 10^3$ 11.4×10^2 $5.9 \div 10$ 21.24×10^3

$8.6 \div 10^2$ 7.8×10 $9.21 \div 1$ 13×10^3 $10.5 \div 10^2$

$\bigcirc\bigcirc\bigcirc\bigcirc\bigcirc$

Day 1

1. $10 - \dfrac{1}{2} =$ _____

2. $\dfrac{4}{5} + \dfrac{1}{10} =$ _____

3. $\dfrac{5}{6} \times \dfrac{1}{5} =$ _____

4. Benjamin added $1\dfrac{2}{3}$ cups of flour to his mixing bowl and then realized he had put in too much. He took $\dfrac{1}{4}$ cup of the flour out of the bowl. How much flour did Benjamin's recipe call for?

_____

Day 2

Write the matching expressions.

1. 6 times 4 plus 3 times 4

_____

2. $\dfrac{1}{4}$ times 8 increased by 11

_____

3. the sum of 10 and 12 divided by 2

_____

4. $\dfrac{1}{2}$ of 8 minus 2

_____

Day 3

Find the volume.

1. l = 4 centimeters

   w = 6 centimeters

   h = 2 centimeters

   V = _____ cubic centimeters

2. l = 10 centimeters

   w = 8 centimeters

   h = 3 centimeters

   V = _____ cubic centimeters

Day 4

Draw each polygon. Then, list its attributes.

1. trapezoid   _____

   _____

   _____

   _____

2. rhombus   _____

   _____

   _____

   _____

3. parallelogram _____

   _____

   _____

   _____

1. $\frac{2}{7} + \frac{1}{3} =$ _____

2. $1\frac{9}{10} + \frac{1}{4} =$ _____

3. $8 - \frac{4}{9} =$ _____

4. Byron and Vanessa competed in a bike race. After 30 minutes, Byron had finished $\frac{2}{3}$ of the race and Vanessa had finished $\frac{7}{12}$. Who had finished more of the race? How do you know?
   _____

5. Write the matching expression for 4 *divided by 2 plus 2 times 4*.
   _____

6. Find the volume.
   l = 20 inches
   w = 14 inches
   h = 26 inches
   V = _____ cubic inches

7. Find the volume.
   l = 6 inches
   w = 7 inches
   h = 8 inches
   V = _____ cubic inches

8. What makes a rhombus different from a square?
   _____
   _____
   _____
   _____

 Can a parallelogram be a rectangle? Why or why not?

Fluency Blast

Practice using mental math.

6.29×10^4 $106 \div 10^3$ 14.83×10^2 $6.84 \div 10$ 3.48×10^3

$2{,}437 \div 10^2$ 17.748×10 $28.15 \div 1$ 5.49×10^3 $406.9 \div 10^2$

○○○○○

Day 1

1. $4 \div \frac{1}{2} =$ _____

2. $\frac{1}{2} \times \frac{6}{9} =$ _____

3. Find the area of a rectangle with a length of $12\frac{1}{5}$ feet and a width of $4\frac{2}{15}$. _____

4. Beth measured $1\frac{2}{3}$ quarts of cherries. She realized she only needed half of that amount. How many quarts of cherries does Beth need?

_____

Day 2

1. $(1.8 \times 0.5) \times (3.4 + 2.6) =$ _____

2. Rudy's little brother packs 7 toys in his bag. The bag itself weighs 3 ounces. If each toy weighs $1\frac{3}{4}$ ounces, how many ounces does his bag weigh?

_____

3. Eric planted 647 bulbs in his garden. He had to plant the bulbs in rows of 20. How many rows was Eric able to plant?

_____

Day 3

1. Austin buys fencing for his square dog pen that measures 9 feet per side. How many inches of fencing does Austin buy altogether?

_____

2. Robert is making apple cider. If he makes 6 quarts, how many 1-cup servings can he pour?

_____

3. 59,600 mL = _____ L

Day 4

Use the coordinate grid to answer the questions.

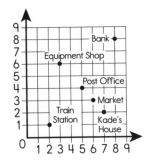

Write the coordinates for each location.

1. Train Station (_____ , _____)

2. Market (_____ , _____)

3. Bank (_____ , _____)

4. What is one path that Kade could take to get from his house to the Equipment Shop?

_____

Name _____

1. Find the area of a rectangle with a length of $4\frac{3}{4}$ yards and a width of $1\frac{1}{16}$ yards.

   _____

2. $8 \div \frac{1}{2} =$ _____

3. $3 \times \frac{1}{6} =$ _____

4. If Fiona's family can drive $23\frac{1}{8}$ miles on 1 gallon of gas, how far can they drive on 17 gallons?

   _____

5. Emma needs 75 ounces of charcoal for her grill. How many pounds of charcoal should she buy? _____

6. Ms. Locklear has 89 yards of string. If she wants to give each of her 15 students an equal amount of string, how much will each student get?

   _____

7. $[(30 - 2) \div 7] \div 2 =$ _____

8. Write the coordinates for the Post Office.

   (_____ , _____)

   What is one path that Kade could take to get from the Equipment Shop to the Train Station? _____

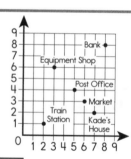

 What are some situations where your math must be precise? When does estimation work better? Make a chart below to compare the two.

Fluency Blast

Practice using mental math.

205.602×10^4 $18.0 \div 10^3$ 39.194×10^2 $38.52 \div 10$ 93.295×10^3

$15.4 \div 10^2$ 289.37×10 $309 \div 1$ 38.53×10^3 $18.3 \div 10^2$

○○○○

Day 1

1. Compare the numbers using <, >, or =.

    0.293 ◯ 0.29

2. Write **five hundred six and twelve hundredths** in standard form. _____

3. Round **122.18** to the nearest whole number.

    _____

4. 9 tens = _____ ones

5. 5.1×10^4 = _____

Day 2

1. $(16 - 7) - (2 \times 4)$ = _____

2. Write a matching expression for 4 *added to 12 times 19 plus 24.* _____

3. Mr. Ortiz gives 9 sheets of paper each to the 6 groups in his math class. He gives 3 sheets of paper each to the 8 groups in his reading class. He has 15 sheets of paper left over. How many sheets of paper did Mr. Ortiz start with?

    _____

Day 3

1. 482 cg = _____ g

2. 51,000 mL = _____ L

3. Find the volume of the figure.

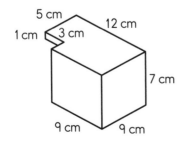

_____

Day 4

Graph and label each ordered pair.
1. A (3, 3)
2. B (7, 5)
3. C (5, 2)

Identify the following points found on the graph.
4. D (_____, _____)
5. E (_____, _____)

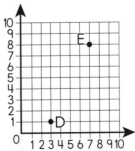

1. Compare the numbers using <, >, or =.

   2,929.87 $\bigcirc$ 2,929.087

2. 6 thousand = _____ hundred

3. Round **26.56** to the nearest whole number.

   _____

4. 25 + (98 − 7) × 4 = _____

5. Write a matching expression for *12 added to 56 divided by 7.*

   _____

6. Whitney completed 25 math problems a day for 20 days. She completed 20 problems a day for 10 days and 15 problems a day for 12 days. How many problems did Whitney solve altogether?

   _____

7. 3,241 ft. = _____ yd.

8. Graph each pair of coordinates.
   (9, 6), (7, 1), (5, 5), (1, 9)

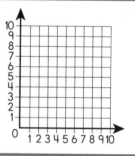

 How would using a table help you solve problem 6? Show how it would work.

Fluency Blast

Practice using mental math.

$3 \div \frac{1}{5} =$ _____ $4 \div \frac{1}{6} =$ _____ $5 \div \frac{1}{3} =$ _____ $4 \div \frac{1}{5} =$ _____ $7 \div \frac{1}{9} =$ _____

$5 \div \frac{1}{4} =$ _____ $7 \div \frac{1}{8} =$ _____ $2 \div \frac{1}{5} =$ _____ $1 \div \frac{1}{5} =$ _____ $3 \div \frac{1}{3} =$ _____

○○○○

Day 1

1. $9.21 + 76.28 =$ _____

2. $175 \times 65 =$ _____

3. $24.50 \div 5 =$ _____

4. $7.09 - 6.99 =$ _____

5. Yvonne watched a video for 0.2 hours in the morning. At night, she continued watching the video for 0.87 hours. How much longer did she watch the video at night?

   _____

Day 2

Rachel's plant grew 2 inches a day.

1. Complete the table.

Days	Growth (in.)
1	2
2	
3	
4	
5	

2. How many inches will the plant have grown by day 8? _____

Day 3

1. Rachel grew a second plant for her experiment. It did not grow the same amount each day. Every day was a different fraction of an inch. Plot the growth on the line plot.

   $\frac{1}{8}, \frac{5}{8}, 1, \frac{1}{4}, \frac{1}{2}, \frac{1}{4}, \frac{5}{8}$

2. How many days did Rachel measure the plant's growth? _____

3. What was the average growth for the plant over the week? _____

Day 4

List the coordinates for each student's house.

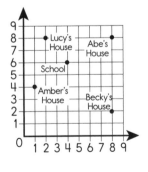

1. Amber's House
   (_____ , _____)

2. Lucy's House
   (_____ , _____)

3. Becky's House
   (_____ , _____)

4. Abe's House
   (_____ , _____)

5. Give a set of directions to get from Becky's house to Lucy's house. _____

   _____

1. Rachel's second plant still did not grow at regular increments. In week 2, it grew much quicker. Use the data to create a line plot.

   $1\frac{3}{4}$, $1\frac{1}{2}$, $1\frac{3}{4}$, $1\frac{1}{4}$, 1, $1\frac{3}{4}$, 2

---

2. Bridget spends 8.45 hours per week watching TV and 6.5 hours per week practicing the piano. Each week, how much more time does she spend watching TV?

   _____

3. $232 \times 0.92 =$ _____

---

4. $4 \times (3.4 + 2) - (56 \div 7) =$ _____

5. Rachel's third plant only grew 1 inch every 2 days. Complete the table to show how much the third plant grew.

Days	Growth (in.)
1	1
3	
5	
7	
9	

---

6. $2.1 + 0.25 =$ _____

   $0.87 - 0.4 =$ _____

7. Find the coordinates for the school.

   (_____ , _____)

   Give a set of directions to get from school to Becky's house. _____
   _____

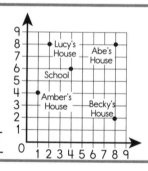

Sometimes we see numbers in problems or stories that aren't realistic. How do you judge if numbers are appropriate for a situation or not?

Fluency Blast

Practice using mental math.

$\frac{1}{5} \div 5 =$ _____ $\frac{1}{6} \div 3 =$ _____ $\frac{1}{3} \div 7 =$ _____ $\frac{1}{5} \div 2 =$ _____ $\frac{1}{3} \div 4 =$ _____

$\frac{1}{7} \div 5 =$ _____ $\frac{1}{5} \div 4 =$ _____ $\frac{1}{4} \div 6 =$ _____ $\frac{1}{3} \div 8 =$ _____ $\frac{1}{4} \div 7 =$ _____

○○○○

Day 1

1. $\frac{2}{3} + \frac{2}{13} =$ _____

2. $\frac{6}{15} + \frac{9}{12} =$ _____

3. $\frac{6}{13} - \frac{2}{6} =$ _____

4. Nina's recipe says to sift $\frac{5}{8}$ teaspoon of baking powder with $\frac{1}{3}$ teaspoon of salt. How many teaspoons does Nina sift altogether?

   _____

Day 2

1. $5 \times (5 - 3) =$ _____

2. $20 - (4 \times 3) =$ _____

3. $(7 \times 8) - (4 \times 9) =$ _____

4. $8 + 6 \div 2 - 2 =$ _____

5. $12 \div 2 + 15 - (144 \div 9) =$ _____

Day 3

1. A company measured its cereal box. What is the volume if the dimensions are 2 inches long, 14 inches high, and 3 inches wide? _____

2. A baby's block measures 12 centimeters on all sides. What is the block's volume? _____

3. A juice box measures 4 centimeters long, 10 centimeters high, and 5 centimeters wide. What is the volume of juice? _____

4. The dimensions of a toy box are 2 feet high, 2 feet wide, and 3 feet long. What is the box's volume? _____

Day 4

Complete the chart for quadrilaterals.

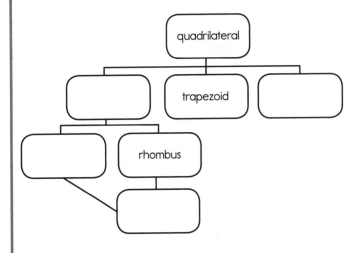

Name _____

1. $\dfrac{3}{8} + \dfrac{2}{3} =$ _____

2. $1\dfrac{1}{7} - \dfrac{1}{3} =$ _____

3. $\dfrac{7}{15} + \dfrac{2}{3} =$ _____

4. The basketball team ordered two pizzas. They had $\dfrac{1}{3}$ of one and $\dfrac{1}{4}$ of the other left over. What fraction of the pizza was left?

    _____

5. $6 \times 5 - 5 \times 4 =$ _____

6. $(5 \times 3) \div 5 + 12 =$ _____

7. Nicole and her friend are building a wooden frame for a garden. They want it to measure 10 feet long, 5 feet wide, and 1 foot high. What volume of dirt will it be able to hold?

    _____

8. The shed in Kevin's yard is 16 yards long, 4 yards wide, and 5 yards high. How much space is inside the shed?

    _____

 Make a hierarchy chart for all polygons.

Fluency Blast

Practice using mental math.

$\frac{1}{4} \div 8 =$ _____ $12 \div \frac{1}{6} =$ _____ $4 \div \frac{1}{8} =$ _____ $\frac{1}{2} \div 4 =$ _____ $\frac{1}{9} \div 3 =$ _____

$\frac{1}{3} \div 9 =$ _____ $8 \div \frac{1}{2} =$ _____ $6 \div \frac{1}{3} =$ _____ $\frac{1}{7} \div 4 =$ _____ $4 \div \frac{1}{10} =$ _____

○○○○

Day 1

1. $\frac{3}{4} \div \frac{1}{2} =$ _____

2. $\frac{1}{3} \times \frac{2}{5} =$ _____

3. Shade the area on the grid that shows $\frac{7}{8} \times \frac{3}{4}$.

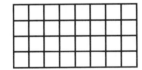

4. Of the shoes in Liza's closet, $\frac{1}{2}$ are sandals. Of the sandals, $\frac{1}{2}$ are brown. What fraction of Liza's shoes are brown sandals? _____

Day 2

1. The Equipment Shop sold 950 golf balls in buckets. If each bucket holds 100 golf balls, how many buckets did the store sell? _____

2. Jonathon's bakery has 1,294 cups of frosting. If each cake he frosts uses 2 cups of frosting, how many cakes can he frost? _____

3. Mrs. Irving's class ate $\frac{1}{5}$ of their green pepper pizza and $\frac{9}{12}$ of their pepperoni pizza. Which pizza did they eat more of? Explain. _____

_____

Day 3

1. Find the volume.

   $l = 4.5$ m

   $w = 3$ m

   $h = 8.5$ m

   $V =$ _____

2. Find the volume of the figure. _____

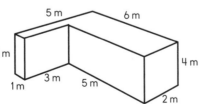

3. A new sandbox measures 12 feet long, 1 foot high, and 6 feet wide. What volume of sand can it hold? _____

Day 4

1. Graph the coordinates. Connect them in the order they are listed.

   (2, 6) and (4, 4)

   (4, 4) and (6, 6)

   (4, 4) and (4, 1)

   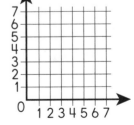

2. What letter did you make? _____

---

1. Gregory's scooter uses $\frac{1}{4}$ gallon of fuel each mile. If Gregory drives 2 miles, how much fuel does he use? _____

2. $\frac{2}{3} \times \frac{5}{7} =$ _____

3. $\frac{4}{6} \times 12 =$ _____

4. $4 \div \frac{1}{4} =$ _____

5. $\frac{1}{10} \div 3 =$ _____

6. If 4 people share a 25-pound bag of potatoes equally, how many pounds of potatoes should each person get? _____

7. Find the volume.

   l = 5 centimeters

   w = 5 centimeters

   h = 7 centimeters

   V = _____ cubic centimeters

8. Graph the coordinates. Connect them in the order they are listed.
   (2, 5) and (6, 5), (6, 5) and (2, 1), (2, 1) and (6, 1)

   What letter did you make? _____

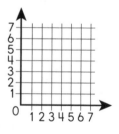

 How would you solve problem 6 differently if the weight of potatoes were tripled?

Answer Key

Page 9
Fluency Blast: 8, 5, 36, 4, 27, 5, 72, 10, 10, 48, 2, 4;
Day 1: 1. 0.04; 2. 20,000; 3. <; 4. 5.7; 5. 40;
Day 2: 1. 23; 2. 12; 3. 7 inches; **Day 3:** 1. 6,000;
2. 200; 3. 0.5; 4. 4 yards; **Day 4:** 1–3. Check
students' work. 4. (3, 7); 5. (8, 2)

Page 10
1. 5,000; 2. 45; 3. >; 4. 30; 5. 260; 6. 175 cans;
7. 45 in.; 8. Check students' work.

Page 11
Fluency Blast: 42, 9, 16, 2, 28, 27, 14, 9, 12, 2, 63,
15; **Day 1:** 1. 10; 2. 127; 3. 73.71; 4. $13.42; 5. $62.52;
Day 2: 1. 30, 45, 60, 75; 2. day 20; **Day 3:** 1. 1/8, 1/8,
1/4, 1/4, 1/4, 1/3, 1/3, 1/3, 1/3, 1/2, 1/2, 1/2; 2. Check
students' work. 3. 1/3; 4. 1/8; **Day 4:** 1. Check
students' work. 2. day 40

Page 12
1. 88, 5; 2. $3.73; 3. $51.72; 4. $6.02; 5. 7;
6. Check students' work. 7. 3, 4, 5, 6; 8. Check
students' work.

Page 13
Fluency Blast: 32, 5, 20, 12, 18, 6, 63, 8, 6, 5, 8, 42;
Day 1: 1. 27 11/12 min.; 2. 7/8; 3. 5/6; 4. 1/12; 5. 40;
Day 2: $7.12; 2. 34; 3. (2 × 7) – (3 × 1);
Day 3: 1. 5,000; 2. 2.5; 3. 48,000; 4. 8,000 grams;
Day 4: 1. Check students' work. 2. 4 right angles,
2 sets of parallel sides, 2 sets of equal-length sides

Page 14
1. 2/3; 2. 7/8; 3. 7/8 cup; 4. 77; 5. 2.38; 6. >; 7. 6;
8. 2 sets of parallel sides, opposite angles are
congruent

Page 15
Fluency Blast: 18, 8, 20, 4, 54, 24, 27, 7, 35, 90, 8, 16;
Day 1: 1. 5/8; 2. 11/20; 3. 1/9; 4. 84.15; 5. 28.05;
Day 2: 1. 98 square yards; 2. $12.40; 3. (9 × 5) – 15;
Day 3: 1. 13 sticks; 2. 10 sticks; 3. 10 sticks;
Day 4: 1. rectangle, square, rhombus

Page 16
1. 73.71; 2. Check students' work. 3. 11.59; 4. 1 3/4 oz.;
5. 144 lb.; 6. Check students' work. 7. 14 sticks;
8. scalene, isosceles, equilateral

Page 17
Fluency Blast: 20, 6, 21, 8, 40, 7, 15, 7, 60, 9, 14, 6;
Day 1: 3.05; 2. 0.036; 3. 2,000; 4. >; 5. 980,507;
Day 2: 1. (4 × 5) + 12; 2. 2 × (4 × 7); 3. $81;
Day 3: 1. 24; 2. 5,280; 3. 36; 4. 8,500 m;
Day 4: 1–3. Check students' work. 4. (1, 5); 5. (4, 3)

Page 18
1. >; 2. 9.92; 3. 0.11; 4. (4 × 4) + (2 × 5); 5. 0.9;
6. 48 qt.; 7. 1.2; 8. Check students' work.

Page 19
Fluency Blast: 28, 18, 24, 18, 8, 25, 5, 36, 7, 56, 9, 4;
Day 1: 1. 132; 2. 928; 3. 20.7; 4. $2.50;
Day 2: 1. 57, 58, 59, 60; 2. 73; **Day 3:** 1. Check
students' work. 2. 1/4 hour, 3/4 hour; 3. 1/2 hour;
Day 4: 1. (7, 2); 2. (1, 7); 3. (4, 3); 4. (5, 6)

Page 20
1. Check students' work. 2. $254.83; 3. 1,000;
4. 13.1; 5. 56, 57, 58, 59, 60; 6. 336, 81; 7. Check
students' work.

Answer Key

Page 21
Fluency Blast: 36, 4, 30, 81, 6, 8, 36, 12, 5, 12, 6, 64;
Day 1: 1. 14 1/2; 2. 1/4; 3. 1/3; 4. 1/2 of the apple;
Day 2: 1. 20; 2. 19; 3. 10; 4. 40; 5. 15;
Day 3: 1. 11 yards; 2. 17 in.; 3. 1/2;
Day 4: 1. perpendicular; 2. Check students' work.
3. 2, 2, 0

Page 22
1. No, half of a deck is 26 cards. 2. 1 1/20;
3. 15 3/4; 4. 10; 5. 36; 6. 4; 7. 72 guests; 8. Check
students' work.

Page 23
Fluency Blast: 81, 4, 24, 24, 8, 10, 28, 7, 12, 6, 6, 48;
Day 1: 1. 23; 2. 7/10; 3. 7/10; 4. 1 1/2 hours;
Day 2: 1. 283 1/3 yd.; 2. 1,110 min.; 3. 4; **Day 3:** 1. 500,
800, 1,100, 1,400; 2. 10,000; **Day 4:** 1. rectangle;
2. (3, 4), (5, 4), (5, 7), (3, 7); 3. (3, 3), (5, 3),
(5, 6), (3, 6)

Page 24
1. 29; 2. 7/12 lb.; 3. 5 9/10; 4. 2 1/2; 5. 18 gal.;
6. 15 gal.; 7. 0.38; 8. (6, 1)

Page 25
Fluency Blast: 12, 49, 2, 10, 6, 32, 8, 21, 40, 4, 54, 8;
Day 1: 1. three and six tenths; 2. <; 3. 0.005;
4. 300,000; 5. 93.013; **Day 2:** 1. 19.5; 2. 50; 3. 19
seashells; **Day 3:** 1. 4; 2. 13,000; 3. 4; 4. 1 1/4 pt.;
Day 4: 1–3. Check students' work. 4. (6, 10);
5. (9, 4)

Page 26
1. one and eight hundredths; 2. <; 3. 2,000,000;
4. 2; 5. 108; 6. 27 problems; 7. 7; 8. Check
students' work.

Page 27
Fluency Blast: 20, 3, 45, 35, 56, 9, 32, 22, 8, 4, 7, 9;
Day 1: 1. 3,730; 2. 81; 3. 17.11; 4. $10.86; **Day 2:** 1. 9, 10,
11, 12; 2. 17; **Day 3:** 1. Check students' work.
2. 3 people; 3. 7/8; **Day 4:** 1. Check students' work.
rhombus; 2. Check students' work.

Page 28
1. 1/2 pt.; 2. $14.10; 3. 46.9; 4. 0.108; 5. 8, 12, 16, 20;
6. 1,744, 121.69; 7. Check students' work. I

Page 29
Fluency Blast: 2, 6, 2, 6, 12; **Day 1:** 1. 5, 1, 12; 2. 19, 30;
3. 16 1/2; 4. 1 3/8 boxes; **Day 2:** 1. 2; 2. 5; 3. 25;
4. 8; 5. 105; **Day 3:** 1. Check students' work. 2. 3/10,
8/10; 3. 5/10; **Day 4:** 1. isosceles; 2. scalene;
3. equilateral; 4. isosceles

Page 30
1. Check students' work. 4 teaspoons; 2. 3 mi.; 3. 5;
4. 1; 5. 5; 6. 4 1/2, 8 5/6; 7. Check students' work.

Page 31
Fluency Blast: 300, 8,000, 60,000, 400,000, 5,000,
10,000, 200, 7,000,000, 90,000,000, 1,200;
Day 1: 1. 11/15; 2. 1 27/40; 3. 1 1/12; 4. 17/30;
Day 2: 1. 132, 133, 134, 135; 2. 980; **Day 3:** 1. 59 cups;
2. 40 servings; **Day 4:** 1. isosceles triangle; 2. (4, 1),
(6, 1), (5, 5); 3. (9, 4), (7, 4), (8, 8)

Page 32
1. 1/2; 2. 1 1/6; 3. 9/20; 4. 19/21; 5. 1 3/5 walls;
6. 1 11/40 lb.; 7. 14 gal.; 8. Check students' work.
rectangle

Page 33
Fluency Blast: 12, 14, 9, 21, 16, 18, 10, 12, 15, 24;
Day 1: 1. 0.4; 2. 7.4; 3. 0.7; 4. 7; 5. <; **Day 2:** 1. (2 × 9)
+ 27; 2. (108 ÷ 12) + (18 ÷ 2); 3. 14 pieces of candy;
Day 3: 1. 28; 2. 7; 3. 96; 4. 44,140 mph;
Day 4: 1–3. Check students' work. 4. (5, 4); 5. (8, 7)

Answer Key

Page 34

1. 2.2; 2. 5.4; 3. four and two thousandths;
4. (35 − 7) ÷ (9 − 2); 5. 0.32; 6. 48 pages; 7. 252;
8. Check students' work.

Page 35

Fluency Blast: 1/2, 3/5, 4/9, 1/4, 2/3, 1/5, 5/8, 3/5,
1/3, 1/5; **Day 1:** 1. 33; 2. 52; 3. 45.06; 4. 18.5 laps;
Day 2: 1. 26, 27, 28, 29; 2. 54; **Day 3:** 1. Check
students' work. 2. 2/3; 3. 1/2; 4. 2 friends;
Day 4: 1. Check students' work. parallelogram

Page 36

1. Check students' work. No, she only has
2 1/3 feet. She is 2/3 foot short. 2. 23.6 min.;
3. 1/10 lb.; 4. 29; 5. 11, 12, 13, 14; 6. 2,730, 121;
7. Check students' work. trapezoid

Page 37

Fluency Blast: 6, 10, 12, 48, 40, 72, 63, 60, 40, 30;
Day 1: 1. 2 5/24; 2. 10 5/6; 3. 1 1/8 cups; **Day 2:** 1. 36;
2. 11; 3. 0; 4. 52; 5. 80; **Day 3:** 1. 66 pt.; 2. $13.08;
3. 8.01 meters; **Day 4:** Check students' work.

Page 38

1. 1 1/6; 2. 3/20; 3. They have eaten the same
amount. 1/4 = 2/8; 4. 9; 5. 23; 6. 4; 7. 144 inches;
8. Check students' work.

Page 39

Fluency Blast: 8, 12, 2, 10, 12; **Day 1:** 1. 1 1/6; 2. 1 1/15;
3. 7/15; 4. 1/8; 5. 5/8; **Day 2:** 1. 6 times; 2. 249 mi.;
Day 3: 1. 20,000; 2. 5.1; 3. 0.015; 4. 3,500 m;
Day 4: 1. 4 sides, exactly one set of parallel sides;
2. Check students' work. 3. (5, 8) or (3, 0)

Page 40

1. 2/9; 2. 1/12; 3. 1 3/5 sq. ft.; 4. 24; 5. 1/6 of a bottle;
6. 12 gal.; 7. 4.22; 8. Check students' work.

Page 41

Fluency Blast: 240,000, 0.013, 1,600, 8.2, 25,000,
0.16, 820, 25, 1,300, 0.24; **Day 1:** 1. 0.07; 2. 30 + 6 +
0.1 + 0.04; 3. =; 4. 9.75; 5. 7,000; **Day 2:** 1. 4 ×
[(10 − 8) − 3]; 2. (34 − 5) × (16 − 11); 3. 1,005 mi.;
Day 3: 1. 10,560; 2. 540; 3. 15; 4. 20 quarts;
Day 4: 1–3. Check students' work. 4. (1, 7); 5. (10, 9)

Page 42

1. 100 + 8 + 0.9 + 0.02; 2. <; 3. 62.69; 4. 17.4;
5. (16 − 2) ÷ (7 − 5); 6. 188 CDs and DVDs; 7. 8;
8. Check students' work.

Page 43

Fluency Blast: 7/8, 1/4, 5/6, 1/12, 3/10, 4/5, 5/6, 5/9,
1/2, 2/5; **Day 1:** 1. 70,494, 2. 0.822, 3. 26.304, 4. 5.49;
5. 11.035 kmh; **Day 2:** 1. 39, 40, 41, 42; 2. 105;
Day 3: 1. 10 pieces; 2. 7 pieces; 3. 3/10;
Day 4: 1. (1, 1); 2. (5, 8); 3. (7, 7); 4. Answers will vary.

Page 44

1. Yes, the total lengths of all of the strings added
together is less than 5 feet. 2. 4.992 mi.; 3. 0.04;
4. Check students' work. E; 5. 35, 36, 37, 38;
7. 11,556, 8.6; 8. (8, 2), Answers will vary.

Page 45

Fluency Blast: 35, 30, 56, 70, 18, 30, 36, 42, 30, 12;
Day 1: 1. 2/15; 2. 14/15; 3. 9/10; 4. 19/70 of the crop;
Day 2: 1. 9; 2. 21; 3. 15; 4. 44; 5. 70; **Day 3:** 1. 117; 2. 8;
3. 122; 4. 3 1/12 hours; **Day 4:** 1. 8 in.; 2. 16 cm;
3. 9.5 in.

Page 46

1. 2/3; 2. 13/24; 3. Molly's family. 5/6 > 5/8; 4. 56;
5. 10; 6. 6; 7. 15; 8. 13.5 cm

Page 47

Fluency Blast: 3, 10, 5, 9, 7, 18, 15, 5, 7, 6; **Day 1:** 1. 1;
2. 11/12; 3. 5/16; 4. 14/15 pt.; **Day 2:** 1. 12; 2. 5.4; 3. 119;
4. 45; 5. 5.4; **Day 3:** 1. $32.15; 2. 6 hr.; 3. 5;
Day 4: 1. trapezoid; 2. isosceles; 3. kite

Answer Key

Page 48

1. 5 3/5; 2. 12; 3. 1/8 lb.; 4. 1/15; 5. 1/32 of the shirts;
6. 12 mi.; 7. 10; 8. rhombus or square

Page 49

Fluency Blast: 8, 12, 14, 24, 56; **Day 1:** 1. 5; 2. 40 + 1 +
0.3 + 0.02; 3. >; 4. 22; 5. 30.5; **Day 2:** 1. 15; 2. 7;
3. (115 − 3) ÷ 8, 14 pages; **Day 3:** 1. 5; 2. 28;
Day 4: 1–3. Check students' work. 4. (0, 5); 5. (2, 9)

Page 50

1. 23; 2. >; 3. 20 + 8 + 0.9 + 0.03; 4. 13; 5. 16;
6. 133 mi.; 7. 10; 8. Check students' work.

Page 51

Fluency Blast: 990,000, 0.048, 5,400, 6.5, 91,000,
0.44, 890, 17, 37,000, 6.1; **Day 1:** 1. 16,962; 2. 0.505;
3. $21; **Day 2:** 1. 58, 59, 60, 61; 2. 12; **Day 3:** 1. 24;
2. 42; **Day 4:** 1. (0, 8); 2. (4, 8); 3. (4, 2); 4. Check
students' work. 6 blocks

Page 52

1. Check students' work. 9 blocks; 2. $40.79;
3. 56,000; 4. 0.4; 5. 63, 66, 69, 72; 6. 40; 7. 484.61,
18.13

Page 53

Fluency Blast: 8 3/5, 2 7/8, 4 1/5, 7 1/6, 9 2/5, 3 1/11,
3 1/4, 1 3/7, 3 5/9, 2 2/3; **Day 1:** 1. 1/2; 2. 19/63;
3. 1 5/12 qt.; 4. 7/12 of the pizza; **Day 2:** 1. 3 × (2 +
46); 2. 16 + (2 × 9); 3. (29 − 4) × 2; 4. (90 ÷ 9) − 6;
Day 3: 1. 60; 2. 24; **Day 4:** triangle, 3; 4, 4;
pentagon, 5; 6, 6; 7, 7; octagon, 8

Page 54

1. 7/9; 2. 9/10; 3. 12 hr.; 4. (34 − 6) × 3;
5. 5 × (23 + 7); 6. 339 1/2 oz.; 7. 100; 8. 9, 9

Page 55

Fluency Blast: 2, 3, 9, 6, 6, 4, 8, 5, 5, 4;
Day 1: 1. 3 1/3; 2. 40; 3. 6 1/2 sq. ft.; 4. 1 2/3 lb.;
Day 2: 1. 24 bowls; 2. Miguel, 2/6 < 3/8;
Day 3: 1. 64 cubic yd. 2. 216 cubic ft.; **Day 4:** 1. 5 ft.;
2. Check students' work. 3. 9 ft.

Page 56

1. 1/25; 2. 2 sq. in.; 3. 16 servings; 4. 1/5;
5. 6 17/20 cups; 6. 1,000 cubic m; 7. 1,728 cubic cm;
8. Check students' work. (21, 19)

Page 57

Fluency Blast: 23, 11, 2, 13, 5, 6, 9, 71, 11, 12;
Day 1: 1. 2,500; 2. 57.142; 3. 8.9; 4. 9; 5. <;
Day 2: 1. 1/4; 2. 4 × [(10 − 8) − 3]; 3. 3,603 cookies;
Day 3: 1. 60 cubic yd.; 2. 84 cubic mm;
Day 4: 1–3. Check students' work. 4. (6, 4); 5. (2, 0)

Page 58

1. 6.9; 2. 927.15; 3. 150; 4. 24.79; 5. 8 + (23 + 10);
6. 4,505 doughnuts; 7. 56 cubic in.; 8. Check
students' work.

Page 59

Fluency Blast: 28, 15, 44, 30, 20; **Day 1:** 1. 6.78;
2. 27,470; 3. 11.01; 4. $74.71; **Day 2:** 1. 44, 46, 48, 50;
2. 110; **Day 3:** 1. 84 cubic ft. 2. 32 cubic in.;
Day 4: 1. (1, 6); 2. (2, 3); 3. (6, 5); 4. (5, 8)

Page 60

1. 618.73; 2. 35.5; 3. $10.90; 4. 4.556; 5. 30.605; 6. 49,
51, 53, 55; 7. 168 cubic in. 8. (8, 1); Answers will vary.

Page 61

Fluency Blast: 560,000, 0.087, 14,500, 27.9, 25,000,
1.65, 8,070, 309, 13,000, 0.24; **Day 1:** 1. 1 1/2; 2. 1/2;
3. 2 7/8 yd.; 4. 4 7/8 lb.; **Day 2:** 1. 8 + (12 × 4);
2. (200 ÷ 10) − 16; 3. (42 × 3) ÷ 2; 4. 4 × (53 + 11);
Day 3: 1. 288; 2. 200; **Day 4:** 1. 131, obtuse; 2. 40,
acute; 3. 55; acute; 4. 25, acute; 5. 90, right

Answer Key

Page 62

1. 1 1/4; 2. 2/3; 3. 4 2/5; 4. 3/4 hr.; 5. (16 × 10) – 14;
6. 45 + (3 × 12); 7. 576 cubic yd.; 8. 50, acute

Page 63

Fluency Blast: 3, 7, 70, 10, 7, 103, 41, 54, 60, 7;
Day 1: 1. Check students' work. 2. 1/16; 3. 5/6;
4. 2/15; **Day 2:** 1. (3 + 6) × (4 + 3); 2. (16 + 10) ÷ 2;
3. (60 ÷ 5) + 11; 4. (12 × 8) – (54 + 11);
Day 3: 1. 80 cubic in.; 2. 504 cubic in.;
Day 4: 1–4. Check students' work. 5. (7, 2)

Page 64

1. Check students' work; 2. 1/35; 3. 1/7; 4. 1/40;
5. 8 pt.; 6. 585 mi.; 7. 250 cubic in.; 8. Check
students' work.

Page 65

Fluency Blast: 1 3/5, 1 1/2, 1 1/2, 2 5/8, 2 5/6, 1 1/9,
1 5/17, 6 2/3, 1 5/8, 3 1/2; **Day 1:** 1. >; 2. fifty-four and
thirty-nine thousandths; 3. 300; 4. 0.84; 5. 4.77;
Day 2: 1. 2,088; 2. 70 – (20 – 13); 3. 4,406 bagels;
Day 3: 1. 65 cubic cm; 2. 137.8 cubic km; 3. 5;
Day 4: 1–3. Check students' work. 4. (1, 2); 5. (2, 4)

Page 66

1. 9.1; 2. one hundred eighty-seven and
twenty-three thousandths; 3. 27.98; 4. 5;
5. 2/3 × (2/8 + 4/8); 6. 3,188 basketballs; 7. 3 lb.;
8. Check students' work.

Page 67

Fluency Blast: 1 3/5, 3 3/4, 2 1/3, 2 1/2, 3 1/3,
1 1/5, 2 1/7, 2 2/9, 1 1/12, 4 1/4; **Day 1:** 1. 372.34;
2. 116; 3. 80,012; 4. 43.8; **Day 2:** 1. 50, 75, 100, 125;
2. 4 necklaces; **Day 3:** 1. Check students' work.
2. 1/2 ton; 3. 1/8 ton; 4. 5/8 ton; **Day 4:** 1. Check
students' work. 2. (6, 150), (7, 175); 3. 6 necklaces

Page 68

1. Check students' work. 5 cars; 2. 1.81 kg; 3. 5.66;
4. 0.194; 5. 28; 937.5; 6. 12, 18, 24, 30; 7. Check
students' work.

Page 69

Fluency Blast: 12, 280, 5,700, 104, 16, 2,800, 24, 120,
30.5, 3,400; **Day 1:** 1. 1/2; 2. 9 7/8; 3. 1/3; 4. 1 5/8 lb.;
Day 2: 1. 5 × (3 + 3); 2. 6 + (14 ÷ 7); 3. 2 × 3 + 9;
4. (5 × 9) – 2; 5. [(77 + 17) – 6] ÷ 2;
Day 3: 1. 1,188 cubic yd.; 2. 600 cubic in.;
3. 144 cubic m; 4. 4,500 cubic in.; **Day 4:** Answers
will vary but may include: 1. square, rectangle;
2. parallelogram, square, rectangle, rhombus,
trapezoid; 3. square, rectangle, trapezoid.

Page 70

1. 5/16; 2. 8 16/21; 3. 1 4/7; 4. 10 + (15 ÷ 3);
5. (2 + 6) × 4; 6. 2 × (8 – 5); 7. 3/8 cubic m;
8. Answers will vary but may include square
or rhombus; square, rhombus, or rectangle;
parallelogram.

Page 71

Fluency Blast: 0.8, 0.48, 6.3, 0.28, 0.24, 2.4, 0.20, 1.2,
2, 1.5; **Day 1:** 1. 1/12 2. 2/5; 3. 24 friends;
4. 5 5/6 acres; **Day 2:** 1. 47 trolley cars; 2. 5 hr.;
3. 252 in.; **Day 3:** 1. 512 cubic in. 2. 72 cubic cm;
Day 4: 1–4. Check students' work. 5. M

Page 72

1. 1 4/5; 2. 18; 3. 1/48; 4. 20 1/4 mi.; 5. 48 train cars;
6. 28 1/20 hr. or 28 hr. 3 min.; 7. 648 cubic m;
8. Check students' work. (8, 12)

Page 73

Fluency Blast: 0.3, 0.3, 0.04, 0.7, 0.05, 0.08, 0.03,
0.04, 0.9, 0.6; **Day 1:** 1. 40 + 5 + 0.6 + 0.07 + 0.008;
2. 5; 3. 33.0; 4. >; 5. 35,000; **Day 2:** 1. 6; 2. 2 ×
(6 × 2); 3. 827 tennis balls; **Day 3:** 1. 84 cubic mm;
2. 135 cubic yd.; **Day 4:** 1–3. Check student's work.
4. (6, 6); 5. (9, 3)

Answer Key

Page 74

1. 270,000; 2. 8.6; 3. 600 + 50 + 8 + 0.1 + 0.02 + 0.009; 4. 2/3; 5. (4 × 3) + (1 × 1); 6. 215 footballs; 7. 120 cubic cm; 8. Check students' work.

Page 75

Fluency Blast: 0.6, 0.06, 0.8, 0.05, 0.06, 0.5, 0.09, 0.7, 0.8, 0.07; **Day 1:** 1. 0.3; 2. 224.56; 3. 19.74 cm; **Day 2:** 1. 8, 12, 16, 20; 2. 32 books; **Day 3:** 1. 15 pieces; 2. No. She only has 9 inches. 3. 12 1/4 in.; **Day 4:** 1. Check students' work. 2. Week 13; 3. Week 19

Page 76

1. Check students' work. 12 3/8 in.; 2. 4.44 in.; 3. 24; 4. 0.08; 5. 4.14, 12.135; 6. 40, 60, 80, 100; 7. Check students' work. 11 days

Page 77

Fluency Blast: 36,700, 0.068, 1,140, 0.59, 21,240, 0.086, 78, 9.21, 13,000, 0.105; **Day 1:** 1. 9 1/2; 2. 9/10; 3. 1/6; 4. 1 5/12 cups; **Day 2:** 1. (6 × 4) + (3 × 4); 2. (1/4 × 8) + 11; 3. (10 + 12) ÷ 12; 4. (8 × 1/2) − 2; **Day 3:** 1. 48 cubic cm; 2. 240 cubic cm; **Day 4:** Check students' work. 1. 4 sides, 4 angles, exactly one set of parallel lines; 2. 4 sides, 4 angles, all sides equal, opposite angles equal; 3. 4 sides, 4 angles, opposite sides are parallel

Page 78

1. 13/21; 2. 2 3/20; 3. 7 5/9; 4. Byron, 2/3 > 7/12; 5. (4 ÷ 2) + (2 × 4); 6. 7,280 cubic in.; 7. 336 cubic in.; 8. A rhombus does not have to have 90° angles.

Page 79

Fluency Blast: 62,900, 0.106, 1,483, 0.684, 3,480, 24.37, 177.48, 28.15, 5,490, 4.069; **Day 1:** 1. 8; 2. 1/3; 3. 50 32/75 cubic ft.; 4. 1 1/4 qt.; **Day 2:** 1. 5.4; 2. 15 1/4 oz.; 3. 32 7/20 rows; **Day 3:** 1. 432 in.; 2. 24 servings; 3. 59.6; **Day 4:** 1. (2, 1); 2. (6, 3); 3. (8, 8); 4. Answers will vary.

Page 80

1. 5 3/64 square yd.; 2. 16; 3. 1/2; 4. 393 1/8 mi.; 5. 4 11/16 lb.; 6. 5 14/15 yd.; 7. 2; 8. (5, 4), Answers will vary.

Page 81

Fluency Blast: 2,056,020, 0.018, 3,919.4, 3.852, 93,295, 0.154, 2,893.7, 309, 38,530, 0.183; **Day 1:** 1. >; 2. 506.12; 3. 122; 4. 90; 5. 51,000; **Day 2:** 1. 1; 2. (4 + 12) × (19 + 24); 3. 93 sheets; **Day 3:** 1. 4.82; 2. 51; 3. 582 cubic cm; **Day 4:** 1–3. Check students' work. 4. (3, 1); 5. (7, 8)

Page 82

1. >, <; 2. 60; 3. 27; 4. 389; 5. 12 + (56 ÷ 7); 6. 880 problems; 7. 1,080 1/3 yd.; 8. Check students' work.

Page 83

Fluency Blast: 15, 24, 15, 20, 63, 20, 56, 10, 5, 9; **Day 1:** 1. 85.49; 2. 11,375; 3. 4.9; 4. 0.1; 5. 0.67 hr.; **Day 2:** 1. 4, 6, 8, 10; 2. 16; **Day 3:** 1. Check students' work. 2. 7 days; 3. 27/56 in.; **Day 4:** 1. (1, 4); 2. (2, 8); 3. (8, 2); 4. (8, 8); 5. Answers will vary.

Page 84

1. Check students' work. 2. 1.95 hr.; 3. 213.44; 4. 13.6; 5. 2, 3, 4, 5; 6. 2.35, 0.47; 7. (4, 6), Answers will vary.

Page 85

Fluency Blast: 1/25, 1/18, 1/21, 1/10, 1/12, 1/35, 1/20, 1/24, 1/24, 1/28; **Day 1:** 1. 32/39; 2. 1 3/20; 3. 5/39; 4. 23/24 tsp.; **Day 2:** 1. 10; 2. 8; 3. 20; 4. 9; 5. 0; **Day 3:** 1. 84 cubic in.; 2. 1,728 cubic cm; 3. 200 cubic cm; 4. 12 cubic ft.; **Day 4:** from top to bottom, left to right: parallelogram, kite, rectangle, square

Page 86

1. 1 1/24; 2. 17/21; 3. 1 2/15; 4. 7/12 of the pizza; 5. 10; 6. 15; 7. 50 cubic ft.; 8. 320 cubic yd.

CD-104975 • © Carson-Dellosa

Answer Key

Page 87

Fluency Blast: 1/32, 72, 32, 1/8, 1/27, 1/27, 16, 18, 1/28, 40; **Day 1:** 1. 3/8; 2. 2/15; 3. Check students' work. 4. 1/4 of the shoes; **Day 2:** 1. 9 1/2 buckets; 2. 647 cakes; 3. pepperoni, 9/12 > 1/5; **Day 3:** 1. 114.75 cubic m; 2. 60 cubic m; 3. 72 cubic ft.; **Day 4:** 1. Check students' work. 2. Check students' work. Y

Page 88

1. 1/2 gal.; 2. 10/21; 3. 8; 4. 16; 5. 1/30; 6. 6 1/4 lb.; 7. 175; 8. Check students' work. Z

Notes